March Away My Brothers

March Away My Brothers

Irish Soldiers and Their Music
in the First World War

Brendan MacQuaile

LONDUBH BOOKS

For Jim

First published in 2011 by

Londubh Books

18 Casimir Avenue, Harold's Cross, Dublin 6w, Ireland

www.londubh.ie

1 3 5 4 2

Origination by Londubh Books; cover by sinédesign

Printed by ScandBook AB, Falun, Sweden

ISBN: 978-1-907535-24-6

from *The Watchers on Gallipoli (1921)*

George Chester Duggan

The Rearguard

March away my brothers, softly march away.
Lest our dead will hear us, softly take you away.
Oh the night is cold for them, brothers once so gay.
Sleeping dreaming waiting 'til the judgement day.

Cold the stars and cold the wind, cold the grey green waves,
Breaking in the little bays, tumbling through the caves.
Night and day they listen, lying in their graves.
Hearing o'er the wild sweet notes elfin organ-staves.

March away my brothers past the grave yard close.
Let your steps be soft and slow, o'er the wind that blows
Gossamer through autumn air the dark winter arrows,
Hail upon their rough wrought graves stir not their repose.

In deep clefts they rest, or high on hillside strown,
No one near, none saw their end and the grass has grown,
Over what is left of them keeping watch alone.
Vanguard of the armies gone, sentinels unknown.

March away my brothers, comrades hear them reap,
The wide plains of the southland, the wheat haulms gold and
        deep
In visions stretch about you, the Blue Mountains sweep.
Lifting up the Forests-and you are fast asleep.

Listen to the sea-winds, brothers from the west,
Scented with the gorse that clasps close the rounded breast.

Of soft Irish hills: you loved your island's honour best.
God's dreams be near you where you take your rest!

March away my brothers: from Highlands to the combes,
Of Sussex land your dreaming is. Thoughts never-ending looms,
Weave out their visions, and in the haunted rooms
Of memory hang fragrant scents of last year's treasured blooms.

March away my brothers; softly march away:
The waves are hissing round us, the east is turning grey.
The coast, the cliffs are silent. Gone are we all, but they
Watch ever in the stillness that falls o'er Suvla Bay.

Falls on the narrow beaches whose verge is sanctified,
By souls of young Crusaders, who on their guest have died:
For them the bars have vanished, the doors are open wide,
And they have seen their King, go up, the bridegroom to the
       bride.

Looking towards Hellespoint on the European side of the Dardanelles where the first landings took place. The Hellespoint monument can be seen in the distance.

Contents

Acknowledgements

I would like to thank Kevin Myers for providing the foreword for this book.

I am part of a group that calls itself 'The Chaps': we have a particular interest in visiting the battlefields of the First World War. Thanks to the other members of the group for their companionship and support.

I would also like to thank Cormac McConnell for kind permission to reproduce the lyrics of 'Christmas Day 1915'; Eric Bogle for kind permission to reproduce the lyrics of 'No Man's Land'/'The Green Fields of France' and 'And the Band Played Waltzing Matilda'; and Paul O'Brien for kind permission to reproduce the lyrics of 'Serving the Crown'.

I have made every effort to trace copyright holders and would be glad to be informed of any errors or omissions that could be rectified in future editions.

Brendan MacQuaile
October 2011

Foreword by Kevin Myers

The music of the First World War forms a part of the uncon-scious mind of everyone in the English-speaking world. Almost everyone, from Canterbury to Connacht and from Vancouver to Vauxhall Bridge, has a corner of their memory put aside for some musical titbit from these times. Merely to hear a snatch of 'Keep the Homes Fires Burning' or 'Roses of Picardy' is to cause instant if only fleeting sadness.

This is one way in which the horrors of the First World War live on – paradoxically, in a far more potent way for many than does the Second World War. In a way, the First World War remains the war to end all wars: perhaps no other war is remembered so acutely, even by those who have no historical knowledge of it. Brendan MacQuaile has done social historians of this period a great service by rooting some of the Irish experience in this broader context.

The songs that the Irish sang were largely the songs that the British soldiers in general sang – although of course with the particularly Irish exceptions. The tale is almost unbearable in its sadness and its pathos, especially in Ireland, where the veterans were to return to a cold and often hostile reception, following a dramatic change in mood after the 1916 Rising. Brendan MacQuaile's use of real people, from recognisable Irish backgrounds, in addition to telling a particular truth, tells a larger truth that is accessible to all.

Here is one of the greatest tragedies of western civilisation – arguably the greatest tragedy – seen through the music and life story of Dublin families. It is a tale that applies in various ways to families in Istanbul and Calais, Milan and Manchester. It is a tale that was once not told in Ireland. But those days are over. The Irish experience is now seen to be part of a wider experience: and all of it is quite tragic and heartbreaking.

Author's Note

The line 'March Away My Brothers, Softly March Away' comes from a poem by George Chester Duggan in memory of his two brothers who died in Suvla Bay on 16 August 1915 during the Gallipoli campaign. I have borrowed Duggan's poignant words as a title for this book.

There have been many detailed histories written about the First World War, charting its causes and effects, I would not dare even to try to compete. Instead I want to focus on some of the more personal aspects of the conflict and especially on the stark contrasts that became evident: the serene splendour in which the King, Kaiser and Tsar lived, while a young widower from High Street, Dublin gave his life to uphold an ideal which he probably never properly understood: the complete and utter folly of the attempt to 'force the Dardanelles', claiming half a million casualties in one of the most scenically beautiful places on earth.

The characters included in this book are all personally connected to me in at least some tentative fashion and, in most cases, I have interviewed their descendants and have heard them first-hand expressing their hurt and underlying disgust at what happened to their loved ones. A sense of anger remains to this day. I have visited all the battle sites myself and walked the ground, trying to envisage how it looked nearly a hundred years ago and how it felt to be there, surrounded by comrades but in constant fear for your life.

Finally I have included music, my first love, as a backdrop to the plot. It's hard for us, in this age of television and radio, to understand the importance of the singing that went on in the trenches and small theatres in occupied villages. Some of the songs are contemporary to the time and some are more modern attempts to paint history through music and words.

1

The War that Couldn't Be Stopped

The political machinations that led to the outbreak of the First World War in August 1914 – one of the most cataclysmic events the world has ever seen – had been brewing for some years. Eventually everything came to a head in the weeks of early July. The assassination of Archduke Franz Ferdinand in Sarajevo set in motion the idea that Austria could wage a short and mobile war to punish Serbia while Europe was on its summer holidays. The Austrians, led by Archduke Franz Ferdinand, 'the politest man in Europe', regarded Serbia as a threat to the Hapsburg Empire. Serbia had doubled in size after the Balkan war of 1860 and had consistently proclaimed itself leader of the southern Slavs. The question was; would Russia back Serbia and cause a more widespread conflict? This outcome was favoured by most of the military top brass in Germany.

Germany's Kaiser Wilhelm II was reluctant to go to war; he certainly talked the talk on many an occasion but he had always shied away from confrontation when it came to the crunch. The fifty-five-year-old Kaiser felt this was a weakness in his character rather than a strength and vowed not to shy away from a fight on this occasion. 'This time I shall not give in,' he told Krupp, the armaments manufacturer. Germany, were she to succeed in her own aspirations, would have to defeat France quickly before turning her attentions to the east. 'Paris for lunch and St Petersburg for dinner,' Wilhelm proclaimed. This also meant invading the neutral states of Belgium and Luxembourg.

The great European powers of Britain, Germany and Russia were at this time ruled by three cousins. George V, King-Emperor of England, the British Empire and India, Wilhelm II, the last Kaiser, and Nicholas II, the last Tsar. However, by 5 July 1914, the day the Archduke was assassinated in Sarajevo by nineteen-year-old Gavril Princip, control of events was already slipping away from the three cousins.

The Kaiser was attending the Kiel yachting regatta, which had been set up some years earlier to compete with the regatta at Cowes on the Isle of Wight. The Kaiser enjoyed all things English and he was clearly upset by the news of the assassination: 'This cowardly detestable crime has shaken me to the depths of my soul.' The Kaiser had in recent times become quite close friends with Franz Ferdinand and had been hunting with him the week before the momentous event.

The Tsar was with his family on board his yacht, the *Standart*, on his annual Baltic summer cruise. His nine-year-old son Alexis had fallen and damaged his ankle. The child, who suffered from haemophilia, was haemorrhaging badly and his mother Alix was in an extremely anxious state. On top of this the news that Rasputin, a former favourite of the Tsarina, had been stabbed by a 'madwoman', meant that the report of Ferdinand's death went largely unnoticed.

King George was also preoccupied. The issue of Home Rule was heating up in Ireland. Ulster had already claimed that she would 'fight and be right' to avoid being separated from Britain and George was worried that if his British army had to fire on British citizens there would be a 'terrible crossfire', with unthinkable consequences. 'Terrible shock for the dear old Emperor,' he wrote in his diary. The King, Tsar and Kaiser were in many ways very alike and their upbringings similar. They certainly lived a charmed and privileged life, but all three felt the burden of their position heavily and struggled in loneliness to deal with their situation.

When the Austrian government delivered its ultimatum to Serbia on 23 July, the die was cast. Even though Serbia's reply on 27 July was humble and acquiesced to virtually all Austria's demands, it appears that the Austrian and German leaders had already decided a war was required and had begun mobilisation.

At home in Ireland there was much discontent. Dublin had

seen a lock-out and a number of workers killed in riots and other demonstrations during the latter half of 1913. Unskilled workers lived in desperate poverty. Housing conditions were deplorable. Overcrowding was a serious problem, causing disease and infection. Malnutrition was common. The death rate in Dublin was as high as Calcutta and the city's slums were amongst the worst in the world. There were often more than ten families living in townhouses that had been built for one upper-class family in the eighteenth century. Landlords rented them out, room by room, to poor families, and they quickly became slums. Many tenement buildings shared one lavatory in a yard.

On the evening of Tuesday, 2 September 1913, two houses in Church Street suddenly collapsed, burying the occupants. The buildings were four storeys high, with shops on the ground floor. The sixteen rooms upstairs were occupied by about ten families, more than forty people. Rescue parties worked through the night digging people out. Seven were killed in this disaster and many more were badly injured.

This was the backdrop to the war: a Europe dissected by class. As with most other wars it was people from the lower classes who were to suffer most, both at home and in the trenches. Perhaps with social conditions so very poor at home, the possibility of a young man becoming a soldier and travelling to war did not seem such a terrible alternative.

Music

It is hard for us to imagine how important music and singing were a hundred years ago. Our modern times have given us a myriad communication options, from television and radio to mp3 players so small they can fit in your top pocket! At the turn of the twentieth century this was certainly not the case. Music for the masses amounted to sheet music being sold for you to take home and play on your own piano. Hit tunes were often sung out by the sheet music salesman when he entered the courtyard of tenement buildings in Dublin. You could nip down and pick up the latest hit but you had to learn and play it for ourself.

This was the era of the music hall and Dublin had many of them, including the famous Theatre Royal. The Royal hosted many a fine evening of song and dance, with famous performers from the opera stage and the new world of silent film, including a young Charlie Chaplin. Dublin's newly formed Rathmines and Rathgar musical society performed Gilbert and Sullivan's *Mikado* in the Queen's Theatre in 1913 and 1914. The gramophone disc had been introduced commercially in 1889 and the Italian tenor Enrico Caruso was the first artist to reach sales of a million in 1904 with a recording of 'Vesti la Giubba' from Ruggero Leoncavallo's 1892 opera, *Pagliacci*.

By this time Ireland had its own rising superstar. John McCormack was born in Athlone, County Westmeath, in 1884, the fourth of eleven children. After some training with Vincent O'Brien he won the coveted gold medal at the Feis Ceoil in 1903. He embarked on a career that would, by the outbreak of the First World War, make him a household name both in Europe and the US. It is something of an urban myth in Dublin that McCormack shared the Feis Ceoil stage with James Joyce in 1903 but this is untrue. Joyce, the possessor of a fine tenor voice himself, competed in the Feis Ceoil in 1904, encouraged by McCormack, and won the bronze medal. Indeed he might well have won gold but for the fact that he did not take the sight reading part of the contest. He is reputed to have thrown the bronze medal in the River Liffey in disgust. The Antient Rooms building where the Feis Ceoil took place still stands on Dublin's Pearse Street. George Bernard Shaw's mother, Mary, also sang on the stage of the Antient Rooms.

During the time soldiers spent at the front and even while they were in the trenches, music and song played an important role in keeping up their morale. Many of the diary entries of the soldiers refer to the concerts and singsongs that took place in the trenches, perhaps accompanied by a squeeze box or harmonica, and also behind the lines during periods of rest. The Scottish singer Harry Lauder (1870-1950) travelled to the front with his five-piece orchestra, at his own expense, to sing for the troops (see Chapter 4). Many of the small villages and towns in Belgium and France still had intact theatres and these were in use for troop entertainment. If a theatre was not available a makeshift arrangement in a tent or barn would have to suffice. Lauder and many other performers played in such venues.

At the start of the war, record sales slumped disastrously. Initially, HMV stayed in business only by instituting massive pay cuts and turning much of its manufacturing capacity over to munitions work. It took Louis Sterling (1879-1958) of Columbia to recognise that there was a huge potential market for patriotic records, which the company went on to exploit very successfully. HMV caught on to the idea shortly afterwards.

The big hit of the First World War was 'It's a Long Way to Tipperary', which dated from 1912 and had not made much of an impression on its first outing. 'It's a Long Way to Tipperary' is a British music hall and marching song written by Jack Judge (allegedly he wrote it for a five-shilling bet in Stalybridge near Manchester on 30 January 1912 and it was performed the next night at the local music hall). Judge's parents were Irish: his grandparents were said to have come from Tipperary.

The *Daily Mail* correspondent, George Curnock, witnessed the Connaught Rangers singing this song as they marched through Boulogne on 13 August 1914 and his newspaper reported the event on 18 August. This was unusual in itself as soldiers did not normally sing while on the march. Other units of the British army then picked up the song. In November 1914 John McCormack recorded it, helping to contribute to its worldwide popularity.

The song proved easy to parody and there were many trench versions, including the one beginning 'That's the wrong way to tickle Mary' which is reproduced on page 21.

Many performers who had 'It's a Long Way to Tipperary' in their catalogue reissued it once it became a popular hit and those who didn't already have it recorded it as quickly as possible. I have heard tell that the song was performed as part of the Theatre Royal pantomime, *Mother Goose*, in 1913; it was certainly a music hall type of composition but I'm not sure about *Mother Goose*!

Another very successful song, this one written in response to the war, was Ivor Novello's 'Till the Boys Come Home', now better known as 'Keep the Home Fires Burning', which soon featured in the catalogue of every recording label. The song's tremendous success brought Ivor Novello overnight fame, launching a hugely successful post-war career and making him one of the most popular British entertainers of the twentieth century.

Novello was born David Ivor Davies in Llwyn-yr-Eos (Grove of the Nightingale) in Cardiff in 1893. His mother Clara Novello Davies was a singer and founded the Welsh Ladies Choir. In 1916 Novello received a commission as a sub-lieutenant and trained as a pilot in the Royal Naval Air Service. He completed dual flying instruction but crash-landed on his first solo. His second solo flight ended in a more serious crash in which he injured his ankle. The Royal Navy grounded him and he was assigned to clerical duties for the duration of the war.

The versatile Stanley Kirkby recorded 'Keep the Home Fires Burning' (in 1916) and similar songs for many record labels including Edison-Bell's Winner label. Kirkby, a music hall baritone, was particularly well known for a serious of patriotic songs he recorded during the war years such as 'Boys of the Dardanelles' and 'Tell my Daddy to Come Home Again'. He also produced successful recordings of love songs like 'When You Know You're Not Forgotten by the Girl You Can't Forget'. He recorded 'It's a Long Way to Tipperary' and 'Irish and Proud of It Too' in 1915.

After the war Kirkby was one of the most prolific recording artists of the early days of the gramophone. His typical fee was about £90 for six songs, normally recorded in one three-hour session, something the singer could do without breaking sweat. This figure was slightly less than a skilled workman's annual wage at this time. The larger gramophone companies paid very handsome fees to artistes, but few, even the famous Gracie Fields (1898-1979), approached Kirkby's gramophone earnings of £270 during the peak recording months of September to January. Kirkby's pure baritone was an interesting alternative to McCormack's lyric tenor. His diction was excellent and he had a versatility in interpretation that distinguished him from many of the other artists recording similar material at that time. John McCormack recorded his version of 'Keep the Home Fires Burning' in 1917. The sentimentality of the song and McCormack's unique ability to tell a sad tale gave it enormous popularity among families at home rather than among the troops serving on the various wartime fronts.

As a brutal war began, so did a period of great expansion of musical entertainment, from stirring marches to trench parodies, from sad ballads to romantic crooning. The music halls were packed with sing along audiences, parlours were full of families singing together and supporting one another, and frightened and lonely soldiers sang or whistled to stave off terror in the trenches and no man's land.

IT'S A LONG WAY TO TIPPERARY

Words and Music by
JACK JUDGE and HARRY WILLIAMS

Allegro con spirito (♩ = c.a. 116)

1. Up to might - y Lon - don came an Ir - ish man one day, _____
2. Pad - dy wrote a let - ter to his Ir - ish Mol - ly O', _____
3. Mol - ly wrote a neat re - ply to Ir - ish Pad - dy O', _____

It's a Long Way to Tipperary

Jack Judge

Up to mighty London came an Irishman one day,
As the streets are paved with gold, sure, everyone was gay.
Singing songs of Piccadilly, Strand and Leicester Square,
Till Paddy got excited, then he shouted to them there.

Chorus
It's a long way to Tipperary; it's a long way to go.
It's a long way to Tipperary, to the sweetest girl I know!
Goodbye Piccadilly, farewell Leicester Square!
It's a long, long way to Tipperary, but my heart's right there.

Paddy wrote a letter to his Irish Molly-O,
Saying, 'Should you not receive it, write and let me know!'
'If I make mistakes in spelling, Molly, dear,' said he
'Remember, it's the pen that's bad, don't lay the blame on me!'

Molly wrote a neat reply to Irish Paddy-O,
Saying 'Mike Maloney wants to marry me and so,
Leave the Strand and Piccadilly or you'll be to blame,
For love has fairly drove me silly: Hoping you're the same.'

Trench Version

That's the wrong way to tickle Mary, that's the wrong way to kiss.
Don't you know that, over here, boys, they like it best like this?
Hooray pour la France, farewell Angleterre.
Oh we didn't know the way to tickle Mary, but we learned how
     over here.

Daisy Bell

Frank Dacre

Frank Dacre had the idea for this song when he paid tax on a bicycle he had imported from the US. A friend remarked that it was lucky he didn't have a bicycle made for two.

There is a flower within my heart, Daisy, Daisy,
Planted one day by a glancing dart, planted by Daisy Bell.
Whether she loves me or loves me not, sometimes it's hard to tell,
And yet I am longing to share the lot of beautiful Daisy Bell.

Chorus
Daisy, Daisy, give me your answer, do,
I'm half crazy all for the love of you.
It won't be a stylish marriage – I can't afford a carriage,
But you'd look sweet on the seat of a bicycle built for two.

We will go tandem as man and wife, Daisy, Daisy,
Ped'ling away down the road of life, I and my Daisy Bell.
When the road's dark, we can both despise p'licemen and lamps
as well.
There are bright lights in the dazzling eyes of beautiful Daisy Bell.

I will stand by you in wheel or woe, Daisy, Daisy,
You'll be the bell which I'll ring, you know, sweet little Daisy Bell.
You'll take the lead on each trip we take,
Then if I don't do well I will permit you to use the brake, beautiful
Daisy Bell

KEEP THE HOME FIRES BURNING
(Till The Boys Come Home)

Words by
LENA GUILBERT FORD.

Music by
IVOR NOVELLO

There's a Long, Long Trail

Lyrics by Stoddard King, Music by Zo Elliott

Nights are getting very lonely, days are very long,
And I'm growing weary, only listening for your song,
And old remembrances are thronging, through my memory,
Thronging 'til it seems the world is full of dreams,
Just to bring you back to me.

Chorus
There's a long, long trail a-winding into the land of my dreams,
Where the nightingales are singing and the white moon beams,
There's a long, long night a-waiting until my dreams all come true,
And that's the day when I'll be going down,
That long, long trail with you.

Sometimes I think I hear you calling, calling sweet and low,
And I seem to hear your footsteps falling, everywhere I go,
And though the road between us stretches, many's the weary
     mile,
Somehow I forget that you're not with me yet,
When I think I see you smile.

2

Over by Christmas

At the very beginning of the war the fighting was intense but fluid, unlike the later stages of trench stalemate. All through the month of October 1914 battles raged as the German forces advanced towards the Belgian town of Ypres. It was here on the morning of the 29 October on the Menin Road leading towards the straggling, typical west-Flanders village of Gheluvert that a young Adolf Hitler received his baptism of fire. His battalion unit, Reserve Infantry Regiment 16, known as the 'List Regiment' after its commanding colonel, had arrived by train from Augsburg via Lille a few days before. In their first encounter they lost many of their number in four days of fighting. Their situation was apparently complicated by the fact that the Bavarians wore caps rather than helmets and their comrades found their mud-stained uniforms hard to distinguish from British khaki in the smoke and fury of battle. Hitler was an aspiring artist and while in the trenches he painted a number of pictures of various aspects of the scene before him.

Waiting nearby, just south of Wytschaete, were the soldiers of the London Scottish Regiment, eager to become the first territorial infantry regiment to go into action. These young men, like twenty-three-year-old Ronald Colman (1891-1958), later famous as 'Raffles', and a recently married Basil Rathbourne (1892-1967), the actor who later achieved fame as Sherlock Holmes, had, only three months earlier, been working in London offices and banks. The men of regiments like this were the precursors to Field-Marshal Kitchener's 'Pals' brigades, sharing a common social, recreational or professional background.

In the early months of the war German armies flowed into Belgium en route to France. This was to be the most mechanised war yet seen anywhere in Europe. As Christmas 1914 approached, the Germans, who had taken ground, were eventually halted before they reached the town of Ypres. They later withdrew in a number of sectors and sought out elevated positions that could be easily defended. In these areas they dug an extensive trench system which was both deep and well protected, but the early Allied trenches were often hasty creations and poorly constructed. If the trench was badly sited it could become a sniping hot spot. In bad weather – and the winter of 1914 was dire – the positions could flood and fall in. The soldiers were not properly equipped to face the rigours of the cold and rain and found themselves wallowing in a freezing mire of mud and the decaying bodies of the fallen.

During the autumn and winter of 1914, millions of servicemen, reservists and volunteers from all over the continent had rushed enthusiastically to answer Field-Marshal Kitchener's call and the atmosphere was one of holiday rather than conflict. But it was not long before the jovial façade fell away. Armies equipped with repeating rifles, machine guns and a vast array of artillery tore chunks out of each other and thousands upon thousands of men perished. To protect against the threat of this vast firepower, the soldiers were ordered to dig in and prepare for next year's offensives, which most believed would break the deadlock and deliver victory.

The men at the front could not help but have a degree of sympathy for their opponents, who were having just as miserable a time as they were. Another factor that broke down the animosity between the opposing armies was the surroundings. In 1914 the men at the front could still see the vestiges of civilisation. Villages, although badly smashed up, were still standing. Fields, although pitted with shell holes, had not yet been turned into muddy lunar landscapes. It was a combination of these factors that made the Christmas truce of 1914 possible.

Ypres was a busy Belgian town and crossroads with a long tradition of linen manufacture. During the Middle Ages it had a strong connection with linen-producing towns in England and

The Cloth Hall in Ypres

it is mentioned in *The Canterbury Tales*. In Flemish the town is called Ieper, pronounced 'Iper'. The municipality, located in the Flemish province of west Flanders, comprises the city of Ieper and the villages of Boezinge, Brielen, Dikkebus, Elverdinge, Hollebeke, Sint-Jan, Vlamertinge, Voormezele, Zillebeke, and Zuidschote: names that would feature on a regular basis during the fighting in what was to become the Ypres Salient. The British Tommies pronounced the name of the town 'Wipers'.

On the eve of the Christmas truce, British forces, still relatively small in number, were manning a stretch of the line running south from the infamous Ypres Salient for twenty-seven miles to the La Basse Canal. Along the front the enemy was sometimes no more than seventy, fifty or even thirty yards away, so Tommy and Fritz could quite easily hurl greetings and insults to one another. Incidents of temporary truces and outright fraternisation were more common at this early stage: even units that had just taken part in a series of futile and costly assaults were willing to talk and come to arrangements with their opponents. As Christmas approached a truce was arranged for the few hours of daylight on Christmas Eve to enable the opposing armies to bury their dead, who had been lying out in the open since the fierce night fighting of a week earlier.

On 24 December the rain cleared and gave way to clear skies. English and German officers and men were grouped around the bodies of the dead, gathered together and laid out in rows. It was, by all accounts, a ghastly sight. The dead soldiers lay stiffly in contorted attitudes, dirty with frozen mud and powdered with lime. The digging parties each dug a big common grave but the ground was hard and the work was slow and laborious. In the intervals of work and rest the soldiers chatted across the language barrier.

That Christmas Eve, the German trenches were a blaze of Christmas trees and the sentries listened for hours to the trad-itional Christmas songs of the Fatherland. The next day the German officers even expressed annoyance that some of these trees had been fired on, insisting that they were part of what was almost a sacred rite. There was something of a festive mood as Christmas approached and the desire for a pause in the fighting intensified as parcels packed with goodies started to arrive from home.

As well as presents from family came gifts from the state. Tommies received plum puddings and 'Princess Mary boxes', a metal case engraved with the profile of George V's daughter and filled with chocolates and butterscotch, cigarettes and tobacco, a picture card of Princess Mary and a facsimile of George V's greeting to the troops. 'May God protect you and bring you safe home,' it said. The Germans also received a present from the Kaiser, the *Kaiserliche*, a large meerschaum pipe for the troops and a box of cigars for NCOs and officers. Towns, villages and cities and various support associations on both sides also flooded the front with gifts of food, warm clothes and letters of thanks.

The Princess Mary box all British soldiers received at Christmas 1914

The Belgians and French received goodies too, although not in such an organised fashion as the British or Germans. For these nations, Christmas 1914 was tinged with sadness, since their countries were occupied. It is no wonder that the truce, although it sprang up in some spots on French and Belgian lines, never really caught hold as it did in the British sector. With the soldiers' morale boosted by messages of thanks and their bellies fuller than normal and with so much Christmas booty still to hand, the season of goodwill entered the trenches.

A *Daily Telegraph* correspondent wrote that in one part of the line the Germans had managed to slip a chocolate cake into British trenches. Even more amazingly, it was accompanied by a message asking for a ceasefire later that evening so the Germans could celebrate the festive season and their captain's birthday. They proposed a concert at 7.30pm when, they told the British, they would place candles on the parapets of their trenches. The British accepted the invitation and offered some tobacco as a return gift. That evening, at the time arranged, German heads suddenly popped up and the soldiers started to sing. Each number ended with a round of applause from both sides. The Germans then asked the British to join in. At this point, one very mean-spirited Tommy shouted: 'We'd rather die than sing German.' To which a German joked aloud: 'It would kill us if you did.'

On many stretches of the front, the crack of rifles and the dull thud of shells ploughing into the ground continued through Christmas 1914 but at a far lighter level than normal. In other sectors there was an unnerving silence that was broken occasionally by singing and shouting drifting over, in the main from the German trenches. Along many parts of the line the truce was enhanced by the arrival in the German trenches of miniature Christmas trees – *Tannenbäume*. The sight of these small pines, decorated with candles and strung along the German parapets, captured the Tommies' imagination, as well as the men of the Indian corps who were reminded of the sacred Hindu festival of light. It was the perfect excuse for soldiers of both sides to start shouting to one another and singing and, in some areas, to pluck up the courage to meet one another in no man's land.

By now, the British high command, comfortably 'entrenched' in a luxurious château twenty-seven miles behind the front, was beginning to hear of the fraternisation. Sir John French, commander of the British Expeditionary Force, issued stern orders forbidding this type of behaviour. Other 'brass hats', as the Tommies nicknamed their high-ranking officers and generals, made grave pronouncements about the dangers and consequences of parleying with the Germans. However, there were many high-ranking officers who took a surprisingly relaxed view of the situation, believing that a ceasefire would at least offer their men an opportunity to strengthen their trenches. This mixed stance meant that very few officers or men involved in the Christmas truce were disciplined. The attitude of the German High Command mirrored that of the British in its ambivalence.

Christmas day began quietly but once the sun was up the fraternisation began. Again songs were sung and rations thrown from one side to the other. It was not long before troops and officers started to take matters into their own hands and ventured forth. No man's land became something of a playground. Men exchanged gifts and buttons. In one or two places soldiers who had been barbers in civilian times gave free haircuts. One German, a juggler and showman, gave an impromptu, and given the circumstances, somewhat surreal performance of his routine in the centre of no man's land.

Captain Sir Edward Hulse of the Scots Guards described, in a letter to his mother which was published in the newspapers of the time, the approach of four unarmed Germans at 08.30. He went out with one of his ensigns to meet them. 'Their spokesman,' Hulse wrote, 'started off by saying that he thought it only right to come over and wish us a happy Christmas and trusted us implicitly to keep the truce. He came from Suffolk where he had left his best girl and a three-and-a-half horse power motor bike!' Having raced off to file a report at headquarters, Hulse returned at 10.00 to find crowds of British soldiers and Germans chatting together and larking about in no man's land, in direct contradiction of orders. Not that Hulse seemed to care about the fraternisation in itself; he was more concerned with being seen to follow orders. He sought out a German officer and arranged for both sides to return to their lines.

While this was going on he managed to keep his ears and eyes open to the fantastic events that were unfolding. 'Scots and Huns were fraternising in the most genuine possible manner. Every sort of souvenir was exchanged, addresses given and received, photos of families shown, etc. One of our fellows offered a German a cigarette; the German said, "Virginian?" Our fellow said, "Aye, straight-cut," and the German said, "No thanks, I only smoke Turkish!"…It gave us all a good laugh.' Captain Hulse was killed in March 1915.

In many parts of the line on Christmas Day, both sides saw the lull as a chance to get into no man's land, seek out the bodies of their comrades and give them a decent burial. The 6th Gordon Highlanders, for example, organised a burial truce with the enemy. Once this was done the opponents inevitably began to talk to one another. According to a contemporary account by a member of the Highlanders: 'The gruesome business of burying continued but there was still a certain interchange of pleasantries. The German soldiers seemed a good-tempered and amiable bunch. The digging completed, the shallow graves were filled in, and the German officers remained to pay their last respects while a British chaplain read a short service. Friend and foe stood side by side, bare-headed, watching the tall, grave figure of the padre outlined against the frosty landscape, as he blessed the poor broken bodies at his feet. Then, with more formal salutes the men all turned and made their way back to their respective trenches.'

With the truce in full swing up and down the line there was a number of recorded games of soccer, although these were really just kick-abouts rather than structured matches. On 1 January *The Times* of London published a letter from a major in the medical corps reporting that in his sector the British played a game against the Germans opposite and were beaten 3-2. Kurt Zehmisch of the 134th Saxons recorded in his diary: 'The English brought a soccer ball from the trenches, and pretty soon a lively game ensued. How marvellously wonderful, yet how strange it was. The English officers felt the same way about it. Thus Christmas, the celebration of love, managed to bring mortal enemies together as friends for a time.'

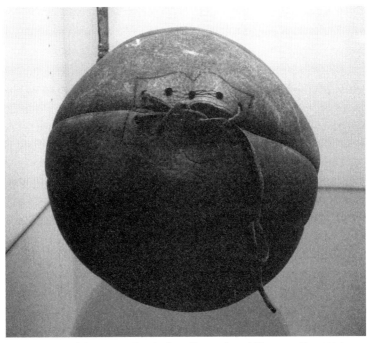

Football of the type used in the friendly matches of Christmas Day 1914

The truce lasted throughout Christmas Day; in places it ended that night, but on other sections of the line it held until 26 December, Boxing Day in England, and in some areas even longer. In fact, there were parts on the front where there was a conspicuous absence of aggressive behaviour well into 1915. Captain J.C. Dunn, medical officer of the Royal Welch Fusiliers, whose unit had fraternised with the Saxon troops opposite and received two barrels of beer from them, recorded how hostilities restarted on his section of the front. Dunn wrote, in a letter that was subsequently published: 'At 8.30 I fired three shots in the air and put up a flag with "Merry Christmas" on it, and I climbed on the parapet. They put up a sheet with "Thank you" on it, and the German captain appeared on the parapet. We both bowed and saluted and got down into our respective trenches, and he fired two shots in the air, and the war was on again.'

The war was indeed on again, for the truce had no hope of being maintained. Despite the fact that it was widely reported in Britain and, to a lesser extent, in Germany, the military authorities and the populations of both countries were still keen to prosecute the conflict. A meeting of enemies as friends over a brief period was not that unusual in the type of trench warfare that existed early during the First War. In Gallipoli the distance between the trenches was down to no more than a few yards at times, so the soldiers had no trouble contacting the other side. But the Christmas truce of 1914 must have had a special feel to it because the men themselves had been told, or at least it had been widely suggested that they would be home for Christmas. When they met their opposite numbers on the German side they must have noticed that the German soldiers were young men themselves with similar hopes and aspirations – and no horns! They certainly would have had much more in common with the Fritzes than they would with the officer corps of their own army. It was heartening to think that they could lay down their arms and celebrate: maybe humanity stood a chance after all.

Cormac McConnell's song is a modern reflection on the Christmas truce in the trenches:

Christmas Day 1915

Cormac McConnell

1915 on Christmas Day,
On the western front the guns all died away,
And, lying in the mud on bags of sand,
We heard the German sing from no man's land.
He tenor voice so pure and true,
The words were strange but every note we knew,
Soaring o'er the living, dead and dammed,
The German sang of peace from no man's land.

They left their trenches and we left ours,
Beneath tin hats the smiles bloomed like wild flowers,
With photos, cigarettes and bottles of wine,
We built a soldier's truce on the front line.
Their singer was a lad of twenty-one,
We begged another song before the dawn,
And sitting in the mud and blood and fear,
He sang again the song all longed to hear.

Chorus
Silent night, no cannons roar,
A king is born of peace for ever more,
All's calm, all's bright,
All brothers hand in hand,
In nineteen and fifteen in no man's land.

And in the morning all guns boomed in the rain,
And we killed them and they killed us again,
At night they charged, we fought them hand to hand,
And I killed the boy that sang in no man's land.

Chorus
Silent night, no cannons roar,
A king is born of peace for ever more,
All's calm, all's bright,
All brothers hand in hand,
And that young soldier sings,
And the song of peace still rings,
Though the captains and all the kings,
Built no man's land.

Stille Nacht/Silent Night

Franz Gruber

Stille Nacht, heilige Nacht/Silent night, holy night,
Alles schläft; einsam wacht/All is calm; all is bright.
Nur das traute hochheilige Paar/Round yon virgin Mother and
     Child,
Holder Knabe im lockigen Haar/Holy infant so tender and mild
Schlaf in himmlischer Ruh/Sleep in heavenly peace!
Schlaf in himmlischer Ruh/Sleep in heavenly peace!

Stille Nacht, heilige Nacht /Silent night, holy night,
Hirten erst kundgemacht/Shepherds quake at the sight.
Durch der Engel Halleluja/Glories stream from heaven afar,
Tönt es laut bei Ferne und Nah/Heavenly hosts sing Alleluia;
Christ, der Retter ist da/Christ the Saviour is born!
Christ, der Retter ist da/Christ the Saviour is born!

3

After the Ball

The Christmas truce was one of the more unusual events of the First World War. It also marked an end to the idea of a 'gentleman's war'. As the year 1915 progressed there were many ungentlemanly new ideas put forward. This year saw the German army first introducing mustard gas, which produced ghastly injuries and deaths, killing from the inside out. The Allies turned their attention to Gallipoli and this short but intense campaign brought different horrors due to the heat and consequent dehydration. It is a chilling thought that your great-grandfather may have drowned, having fallen into a cess pit, while suffering from dysentery and without sufficient strength to pull himself out. This is the type of episode that soldiers in the front line saw and endured but that they never spoke about once they went home after the war. How could you discuss this type of event with someone back home, a loved one, or a neighbour?

Another unusual event of this second year of war involved the 'football team' of the London Irish Rifles, who fought with great skill and bravery during the battle of Loos in September-October 1915 (the first time the British used gas). This involved a group of soldiers who decided to dribble six footballs across no man's land and use the German trench as a goal. Unfortunately for the footballers, their commanding officer found the footballs just before kick-off and managed to shoot and puncture five balls in order to prevent the crazy stunt. Not to be denied their sport, the troops managed to keep one ball ready to roll and when the whistle sounded for the off, their captain, Sergeant Frank Edwards, kicked off with the call of 'on the ball London Irish'. He dashed away, dribbling the football for about twenty yards towards the German line until enemy fire wounded him in the thigh. A number of other soldiers from the regiment took over, passing the ball as they went. Sadly the ball ended up stuck on the wire and burst, putting an end to the game. A silly place to have barbed wire, in the middle of a football pitch!

The happy ending meant that the ball and the story passed into the folklore of the London Irish Brigade. The football, having been retrieved from the barbed wire of no man's land, eventually ended up in the regimental museum where it stayed quietly until it was discovered and used as a centrepiece for the regiment St Patrick's Day parade. I'm not sure if the London Irish football team got a chance to play football with the Germans during the Christmas truce but they were clearly interested in scoring a goal against them during the battle of Loos, which cost many lives on both sides and eventually resulted in victory for the British.

Music

The emergence of a commercial popular-music industry in the US in the 1890s was based on the sales of sheet music, not gramophone records, which did not become commercially available in the late 1890s. Sheet music enabled consumers to play and sing songs in their own parlours and played a big part in ensuring that the soldiers of the First World War soldiers were in a position to sing for themselves. It is unlikely that this would be the case today as we tend to listen to popular music rather than perform it, often locking ourselves into our own little worlds with our iPods.

Sheet music sales rocketed during the 'Gay Nineties,' with Tin Pan Alley, a narrow street in midtown Manhattan, housing the country's major music publishers and producers, blazing a trail. Tin Pan Alley dates back to about 1885 but achieved national prominence only with the first 'platinum' song in American music history. Two million copies of the sheet music of 'After the Ball', a song by Charles K. Harris, were sold in 1892 alone. 'After the Ball' is a classic waltz. In the song, an older man tells his niece why he has never married. He saw his sweetheart kissing another man at a ball and refused to listen to her explanation. Many years later, after the woman had died, he discovered that the man was her brother. The song's emotional appeal eventually helped to sell over five million copies of the sheet music, making it the biggest hit in Tin Pan Alley's long history and a popular choice with the lovelorn troops in the trenches. The song also features in a number of films and musicals, including Jerome Kearns's *Showboat*, in which it was sung by Kathryn Grayson.

One of the lines of the song appears on the gravestone of Hugh Gordon Langton, a British officer killed in Passchendaele in 1917. The musical notation on the bottom of the stone has long been a subject of interest and it seems that the notation is that of the line 'many a heart is aching'.

It is a fitting tribute by the family of Hugh Gordon Langton. He was an exceptionally gifted violinist who, before the First World War, studied under some of the best teachers in Europe but died before he had a chance to achieve international fame. He is commemorated in Poelcapelle British Cemetery. Very little is known about him except that he was a second lieutenant with the London regiment of the Royal Fusiliers and was married before the war. His father, devastated by the loss of his son, became ill and died exactly a week after the First World War ended.

Victor Silvester (1900-78), the famous band leader, played this song on many occasions. When the war broke out, Victor was a boy of fifteen. He ran away from his boarding school and unbeknownst to his parents signed up to fight on the western front. His parents suspected he had enlisted but it was not until 1917, when he was wounded and repatriated, that they found out for sure. In an interview he gave just before his death in 1978, Victor Silvester described how he was ordered to execute a man for desertion:

'The victim was brought out from a shed and led struggling to a chair to which he was then bound and a white handkerchief placed over his heart as our target area. He was said to have fled in the face of the enemy.

'The tears were rolling down my cheeks as the victim tried to free himself from the ropes attaching him to the chair. I aimed blindly and when the gun smoke had cleared away we were further horrified to see that, although wounded, the man was still alive. Still blindfolded, he was attempting to make a run for it, still strapped to the chair. The blood was running freely from a chest wound. An officer in charge stepped forward to put the finishing touch with a revolver held to the poor man's temple.

'He had only once cried out and that was when he shouted the one word "Mother". He could not have been much older than me. We were told later that he had in fact been suffering from shell shock, a condition not recognised by the army at the time. Later I took part in four more such executions.'

Soldiers who could not stand the thought of being on the front line any longer deserted. If they were caught they were court martialled and, if sentenced to death, shot by a twelve-man firing squad. Senior military commanders would not accept a soldier's failure to return to the front line as anything other than desertion. They also believed that if such behaviour was not harshly punished, others might be encouraged to do the same and the whole discipline of the British army would collapse. Some men faced a court martial for other offences but the majority stood trial for desertion from their post: 'fleeing in the face of the enemy'. The court martial was usually carried out with some speed and the execution followed shortly afterwards, usually early the next morning

Few soldiers wanted to be in a firing squad. Many were soldiers at a base camp recovering from wounds that stopped them from fighting at the front but did not preclude them from firing a Lee Enfield rifle. Some of those in firing squads were under the age of sixteen, as were some of those who were shot for 'cowardice'. James Crozier from Belfast was shot at dawn for desertion – he was just sixteen. Before his execution, Crozier was given so much rum that he passed out. He had to be carried, semi-conscious, to the place of execution. Officers at the execution later asserted that there was a very real fear that the men in the firing squad would disobey the order to shoot.

Shell shock was a result not only of the terror and anxiety of serving in the trenches so close to death, but of the sheer exhaustion that came from spending long periods without proper rest in terrible conditions. The British army authorities understood nothing of it at the beginning of the war and cared little for those who appeared to be cowardly. This was a man's war.

In all, some three hundred British and Commonwealth soldiers were executed during the First World War. Such executions, for crimes such as desertion and cowardice, remain a source of controversy with some believing that many of those executed should be pardoned if they were suffering shell shock. The executed, mainly of non-commissioned ranks, included twenty-two Irishmen.

All the stories of this type that have survived are heartbreakingly sad. Stories like that of the young Derry lad, disoriented by repeated shelling, who wandered out into no man's land in total confusion and wandered back, five days later, looking for his regiment. The following morning, after being found guilty of desertion, he was executed. A cousin of his became involved in the Shot at Dawn campaign group, which helped to persuade the British government of the justice of pardoning the soldiers who died, having been speedily court-martialled, at the hands of their own colleagues. He pointed out that 'anybody who walks back into his lines again is not planning to desert'. One boy of fourteen was so patriotic he added two years to his age in order to get to the front, only to be shot at seventeen as a deserter, although he was still too young to be officially a member of his regiment.

In 2006, the British government finally recognised that most of deserters during the trench wars suffered from acute mental stress and disorders such as shell shock and should have received medical treatment rather than being executed for cowardice and desertion. The government issued a posthumous pardon to these individuals, as a result of years of lobbying by family members of the deceased.

'Many a heart is aching': the gravestone of Hugh Gordon Langton in Poelcapelle

After the Ball Is Over

Charles K. Harris

A little maiden climbed an old man's knee,
Begged for a story – 'Do, Uncle, please.
Why are you single; why live alone?
Have you no babies; have you no home?'
'I had a sweetheart years, years ago;
Where she is now, pet, you will soon know.
List to the story, I'll tell it all,
I believed her faithless after the ball.'

Chorus
After the ball is over,
After the break of morn –
After the dancers leaving;
After the stars are gone;
Many a heart is aching,
If you could read them all;
Many the hopes that have vanished,
After the ball.

'Bright lights were flashing in the grand ballroom,
Softly the music playing sweet tunes.
There came my sweetheart, my love, my own –
"I wish some water; leave me alone."
When I returned, dear, there stood a man,
Kissing my sweetheart as lovers can.
Down fell the glass, pet, broken, that's all,
Just as my heart was after the ball.'

'Long years have passed, child, I've never wed.
True to my lost love, though she is dead.
She tried to tell me, tried to explain;
I would not listen, pleadings were vain.
One day a letter came from that man,
He was her brother – the letter ran.
That's why I'm lonely, no home at all;
I broke her heart, pet, after the ball.'

4

The Pals Brigades

Lawrence Kelly, a young man from Bridgefoot Street in Dublin, was married to Ellen and they had one child. Lawrence or Larry, as he was known to his friends, worked for Arthur Guinness and Sons at St James's Gate. He had joined the company as a labourer in 1910, earning twenty-two shillings a week, not a bad wage in those days. When he started work at the Guinness site not far from his home he was automatically put on what the company called the 'B' list for a year's probation. While he was on the 'B' list the company withheld a shilling a week from his wages. Before he was promoted to the 'A' list, Larry had to prove himself as a good worker with a steady character.

Larry proved himself and was rewarded with a position on the 'A' list. This brought an increase in his weekly wage to twenty-four shillings a week and, of course, he was given the back money that had been withheld. Although he worked in the engineering department, he moved to Liverpool in March 1916 and started as a stillion man in the forwarding department (a stillion is a stand for vats or casks). He left to join the 16th Division (Irish), a voluntary division of Kitchener's New Army, in May of that year, enlisting in the 47th Company Machine Gun Corps. The machine gun corps were units hastily assembled in war. They did not have the history or pedigree of regular army units such as the Light Horse, and they were disbanded by 1922. The machine gun corps were tough fighting units and not for parades.

Field-Marshal Kitchener's New Army was formed from a flood of enthusiastic men, such as Lawrence Kelly, from all walks of life. Many rushed to 'respond to the call' of the newly appointed minister at the outbreak of the war. Lawrence, on the other hand, had some time to make his fateful decision and it is very likely that he was influenced by other Guinness workers who had enlisted ahead of him.

Horatio Herbert Kitchener (1850-1916), imperial administrator, conqueror of the Sudan and Commander-in-Chief of British forces during the Second Boer War (1900-02), was Secretary of State for War at the beginning of the First World War. He was born in Ballylongford near Listowel in County Kerry and baptised in the little parish church of Aghavallin. The Kitchener family was English and his father, an army officer, had bought land in Ballylongford not long before Horatio was born. His mother died of tuberculosis not long afterwards, in Switzerland, where the family had moved to try to improve her health.

Kitchener's appeal for volunteers was born out of his realisation that the war would not after all be over by Christmas 1914. He called for a 'first hundred thousand' volunteers. More than five times this number responded. There were many reasons for this. Some were motivated by a sense of duty, genuinely believing that they should serve king and country in the hour of need. Others were motivated by the prospect of adventure abroad and escape from the drudgery and poverty of the industrial towns and mines of early 20th century Britain. Many simply joined up on the spur of the moment because their friends had done so. Whatever the reason, within a few days the city, town and village communities of Britain and Ireland were half a million men fewer and the battalions of Kitchener's New Army were beginning to form their unique character and shape.

In Ireland the workers' strike and lock-out of 1913 had left a very depressed economic situation. It is ironic, however, that most of the early pals volunteers came from a sector of the Irish population whose members were working and had a reasonable income. Whatever the reasons or circumstances, the numbers of Irishmen who enlisted had grown to nearly 150,000 by the end of the war. Amongst the European powers, only the British army was composed almost entirely of volunteers at the outbreak of the war. This meant that it was different in both size and structure from its Continental counterparts. Although the British standing army was well trained and disciplined it was relatively small: hence the call for volunteers by Kitchener.

Some eight hundred Irish mens who worked for Guinness served in the First World War and a hundred and three did not return home. A number of the northern English pals brigades such as the Tyneside Irish were predominantly composed of Irish volunteers.

The basic infantry unit of the British army was (and still is) the battalion, consisting of roughly a thousand men, including thirty-six officers. Of these roughly eight hundred would provide the fighting strength, leaving two hundred support personnel – clerks, signallers, cooks and stretcher-bearers. The battalion was split up into four companies of two hundred and fifty men, which in turn were divided up into four platoons of sixty and the platoons into four sections of fourteen private soldiers and an NCO. To form a whole basic infantry unit – a battalion – became a natural goal for enthusiastic individuals up and down the land, usually factory owners, town mayors or landowners, who took it upon themselves to recruit on behalf of Kitchener and the cause. Many battalions were therefore formed of men from the same area, town, village or even workplace (Guinness for instance) and gave the New Army its unique characteristic, the pals battalions.

In retrospect, it is easy to see that, whilst the pals battalions had tremendous advantages in terms of morale and teamwork, a fundamental flaw underpinned their creation. In 1914, it was assumed that the war would be mobile and over quickly. As we now know, it was neither. This had tragic consequences for small communities whose menfolk went en masse into an attack against machine guns.

The appalling reality of a postman arriving in a local area or street with not one but many letters announcing the death of a father or son forced the authorities to change their ideas on pals brigades and thereafter they separated local men to prevent this situation occurring too often. Interestingly, telegrams were only for the families of officers: the ordinary ranks simply got a buff-coloured envelope, which might have held a gas bill but instead brought the ghastly news that a loved one was dead or missing.

In Ireland the situation was similar to Britain as many of the young Irish volunteers enlisted in the Irish regiments, such as the Dublin Fusiliers, the Ulster Rifles and the Connaught Rangers and entered the war together. The president of the Irish Rugby Football Union, F.H. Browning, issued a circular to Dublin clubs in 1914 encouraging members to join up and an IRFU volunteer corps was formed. In Lansdowne Road almost two hundred men enlisted in D Company of the 7th battalion of the Dublin Fusiliers. Major Irish companies, including Guinness and Bank of Ireland, released staff who volunteered to serve in the war and subsequently maintained rolls of honour recording their names and often their deaths.

It appears that at the end of July the 16th division in which Larry Kelly served was in reserve as part of Sir Herbert Plumer's Second Army. These forces had been involved in the Battle of Messines in mid-June and were supporting Gough's Fifth Army during the Battle of Pilkem at the beginning of August

Larry Kelly served for only a few days at the front. He was killed near Ypres, probably during the Battle of Pilkem Ridge that was fought from 31 July to 2 August 1917). He is remembered on the Menin Gate with 58,000 other soldiers whose bodies were never identified.

The British army issued an edict at the beginning of the First World War that men would be interred where they fell, regardless of rank or status. (In past times well-to-do officers would often be repatriated for burial in family plots, sometimes sent home in a barrel of brandy.) Flanders, in particular, is dotted with small graveyards and even some individual graves. It is very likely that these spots marked a gap in the barbed wire where troops were attempting to break through. It's entirely possible that Lawrence Kelly was killed by a shell, or worse still, he may have drowned in a shell hole, wounded and unable to crawl free of the ever-present mud. 31 July had started fine, but by late afternoon there was a widespread downpour.

The Menin Gate in Ypres was built after the war as a memorial to those whose bodies were never identified. The last post sounds in remembrance there each evening.

AD MAIOREM DEI GLORIAM
HERE ARE RECORDED NAMES
OF OFFICERS AND MEN WHO FELL
IN YPRES SALIENT BUT TO WHOM
THE FORTUNE OF WAR DENIED
THE KNOWN AND HONOURED BURIAL
GIVEN TO THEIR COMRADES
IN DEATH

Inscription on the Menin Gate, commemorating soldiers 'to whom the fortune of war has denied the known and honourable burial'

LANCE SERJEANT
PITTS W.

CORPORAL

ARCULUS L. J. W.
BIGGS G. W.
CALLAGHAN J.
CORNELL C. H.
DAVIES A.
GLANCY M. J., M.M.
KELLY L.
MARCHANT F.
NOBLE G. C.
PATTERSON J. F.
PAUL J. H. W.
PURCELL W.
RUDMAN A. E. R.
SCOTT B.
SETTLE S. C.
THORNE J.
TREDREA H.
TURNER J. F.
WHITEHOUSE M.G.,M.M.

LANCE CORPORAL

Lawrence Kelly's name inscribed on the Menin Gate

Music

Harry Lauder was born in August 1870 in Bridge Street, Portobello, near Edinburgh, the eldest of eight children. When he was twelve his father died and the family moved to Arbroath, where Lauder's mother had relatives and where he went to work in a mill in 1882. It was here that Harry began his singing career. When war broke out in 1914, Lauder was in Melbourne, accompanied by his son John (born 1890). A captain in the army, John was called back to his regiment, the Argyll and Sutherland Highlanders, but Lauder continued with his tour.

Back in London in 1916, Lauder opened in the review *Three Cheers* at the Shaftesbury Theatre. The finale was the song 'The Laddies who Fought and Won', at the end of which a company of Scots Guards marched on to the stage. It was during this run that he received the telegram telling him that John had been killed in Poiziers on 28 December 1916. (John Lauder was buried in France but there is a memorial to him in Glenbranter in Scotland.)

After his son's death, Harry Lauder was given full permission to entertain Scottish troops wherever they were posted. He overrode War Office opposition and instead of just giving concerts at the bases, sang to the troops at the front line, to the accompaniment of a small five-octave piano specially made for him. Lauder was also active in the recruiting of troops and had his own recruiting band. This band travelled around at Lauder's expense and played to attract a crowd: when enough people gathered, the band marched on to the recruiting office. Lauder made speeches from the stage, encouraging young men to join up. More than 12,000 men were recruited through his efforts. Lauder wrote many of his own songs, including 'Roamin' in the Gloamin', and in the wake of his son's death he wrote the sentimental, very popular 'Keep Right On to the End of the Road'.

'The Irish Laddies to the War Have Gone' (p. 52) was a recruiting song from Canada, dedicated to the 108th Battalion Canadian Irish and sung to the tune of 'The Wearing of the Green'.

The Irish Laddies to the War Have Gone

Frank O. Madden

Now Paddy dear and did you hear the talk that's going round,
That auld Ireland's sons aren't loyal to the core?
And they're murmuring that still there are some Irish to be
  found,
Who have not yet enlisted for the war,
Sure and Paddy dear it's us that know the folly of such talk,
And how all her sons have gone to meet the foe,
Faith there's no one left but childer' and gossoons too young to
  walk,
But even they are drilling for to go.

Chorus
Faith and who can be denying that our Irish lads are there,
Sure they're fightin' and they're dying but they are out to do their
  share,
Arrah! When the war is over, then the story will be told,
How our Irish laddies to the war have gone,
As their daddies did in days of old.

Do you know of any decent fight in all of history,
Where the Irish were not foremost in the fray?
Have you heard of any battles on the land or on the sea,
Where the Irish did not fight and win the day?
Sure you'll find our Irish fighting men in every fighting force,
Where they know they fight for liberty and right.
Faith, they'd rather fight than eat, although they sometimes eat of
  course,
But it's only for to fit them for the fight.

5

Picardy and the Somme

It is said that the rose is in some way connected to the nightingale and that the bird sings every time a rose is picked. The rose was a symbol of silence and secrecy in ancient Rome and the roses in Picardy must have fallen eerily silent on the morning of 1 July 1916. The British tunnelled under the German position and a tremendous explosion rocked the earth as the charges set under the enemy lines went off. When the dust settled the German troops were dazed and deafened but they pulled themselves together and fell back quickly into the large crater that the explosion had formed. They waited.

Today the countryside around the French and Belgian border area is beautiful, with rolling hills and lush pastures. On that fateful day, through the silence, the British soldiers left their trenches near a small wood and began slowly to cover the mile-and-a-half or so of open ground in front of the German line. The enemy troops had by this time regrouped and waited, machine guns ready. The range of the German machine guns at this time was about a mile, and as the British walked forward they were initially masked by the gentle slope of the ground, so the silence persisted until they reached the brow and continued into the path of the intense enemy fire. The number of casualties was enormous: some six thousand young men killed or wounded after the morning's action. Many of them were from the Tyneside Irish Brigade.

In Picardy and Flanders there are graveyards from the Napoleonic wars, the Franco-Prussian War, the First World War, the Second World War: just about every sort of soldier you can think of from all over the world is buried here. Strategically located, it has been a battlefield in European wars for centuries.

As we approach the centenary of this most devastating conflict, many families, my own included, are only now discovering that they have some connection with this history? A friend's grandfather here, a distant relative there, your mother's eldest brother – they seem to come to the surface in order to tell us about the enormous impact of this war. I have been surprised by the feelings I have unearthed when speaking to the descendants of some of the men who served. I have found in some cases what can only be described as anger, dormant but palpable, at the fact that these men in some cases gave up a good job to go and fight for king and country. It would be easy to explain how economics influenced many young Irishmen to make such a decision. But do young men go to war for money? Many of the young Irish lads had probably never been outside their own parish, let alone abroad or at sea. But would you readily make a decision to go to Flanders or Gallipoli, abroad for the first time, in order to kill the enemy? Let's face it, war is about killing; you would be extremely naive to think that you could enlist and avoid such harsh realities. And of course there was the specifically Irish problem with fighting for king and country. Was it our king? I have tried in vain to put myself back into the shoes of some of the young men of the time and to understand their reasoning. I've tried to discount the personal feelings expressed by relatives telling me their stories in order to look dispassionately at the hard facts.

It is dangerous to make comparisons with more modern conflicts fought by more professional armies and in more controlled zones of war. The First World War back in 1914 must have appeared to be just that, a world war. The young conscripts must have realised that their world was changing dramatically. The war that began in 1914 had, because of modern warfare technology, the capacity to sweep through many countries, not only on the European mainland but further afield. Ships, tanks and artillery had developed to allow for battlefields, once dictated in distance and size by how far a man could fire an arrow with his longbow, to be enormous. In all there were just over eight million men involved in the war on the Allied side. They were made up of soldiers from many different nations, at least sixteen in all (not including Ireland, which at the time was listed as part of the United Kingdom).

The total number of casualties in the First World War, both military and civilian, was about thirty-seven million: sixteen million dead and twenty-one million wounded. The total number of deaths includes 9.7 million military personnel and about 6.8 million civilians. The Allies lost about 5.7 million soldiers while the Central Powers lost about four million.

Music

Hours of boredom interspersed with moments of sheer terror were very typical for all soldiers in the First World War trenches. Singsongs were a popular way to pass the time. Each division had a concert party and there are many examples of trench songs or trench versions of other songs. The concerts were held in large tents or barns and most of the acting was done in drag. However there was a couple of young ladies who attached themselves to the 6th Division concert troupe: 'The Fancies'. The girls had slipped through as refugees and were quickly nicknamed 'Glycerine' and 'Vaseline'. No one seemed to mind that they couldn't sing or act and one of them, an innkeeper's daughter, may well have been the original 'Mademoiselle from Armentières' whose attributes featured in the trench song of that name that was so popular with the Tommies.

On another occasion, soldiers found a gramophone playing 'A Little Maid from Flanders' amid the ruins of Ypres – perhaps an omen that Ypres would live again after the war.

Because the lyrics of 'Roses of Picardy' are so evocative and touching it has become something of an urban myth that either the lyricist Fred E. Weatherly (1848-1929) or Haydn Wood (1882-1959), who wrote the music, was in the army in Picardy (site of the battle of the Somme) in the First World War, and that he had a French sweetheart he wished to honour with a poem or a song. This is pure – although lovely – legend.

Weatherly, who also wrote the words of 'Danny Boy' to a traditional Irish air, was sixty-eight when he wrote the song in 1916. Of course he was aware of the tragic events that were taking place in Picardy but the area had been a popular holiday destination for Britons since the early 1900s. As for the roses, well, Picardy had never been particularly famous for roses.

From Weatherly's memoirs and other articles we know that he visited France a couple of time. Apparently he never visited Picardy: nor did he go over to France in the war period.

When asked if his love songs were personal, he said, 'I would have had a busy time and a varied experience. Some are, perhaps. But many of them have been written round the love story of a very dear friend of mine.'

The war seemed to stimulate Wetherly's power of song-writing; in this period, he wrote some of his 'best and gayest songs.'

Haydn Wood never joined the army and didn't go to the Continent during the war. But in July 1916, while the Battle of the Somme was raging, he wrote a letter in which he described wounded soldiers he had just seen at Charing Cross Station. He is thought to have composed the music for 'Roses of Picardy' in November 1916. The tempo signature is marked 'Brightly'.

One might read some allusion to the war in the line 'And our roads may be far apart', but the song seems more about happiness, a love song about a lifelong happy relationship. It is all about the boy and the girl who fall in love and wish to stay together until old age. Weatherly's lyrics cover the whole span of a couple's life and I think this is what makes it so special.

The Irish tenor John McCormack recorded the song after the war was over, in 1919.

Roses of Picardy

Words by Fred E. Weatherly; music by Haydn Wood

She is watching by the poplars,
Colinette with the sea blue eyes,
She is watching and longing and waiting,
Where the long white roadway lies.
And a song stirs in the silence,
As the wind in the boughs above,
She listens and starts and trembles,
'Tis the first little song of love.

Chorus
Roses are shining in Picardy,
In the hush of the silvery dew.
Roses are flow'ring in Picardy,
But there's never a rose like you!
And the roses will die with the summertime,
And our paths may be far apart,
But there's one rose that dies not in Picardy!
'Tis the rose that I keep in my heart.

Roses Of Picardy

Words by FRED E. WEATHERLY
Music by HAYDN WOOD

Tom Kettle

Tom Kettle was the most eminent Irish figure to die on the Somme. A politician, poet and academic, he is buried where he died, in Ginchy. I have visited the Irish memorial on the Messines Ridge, which is in Flanders. The small park and Irish round tower, just like the one on your old school copybook, was opened by President Mary Robinson in 1998. It is a beautifully kept, quiet and reflective spot and a stone tablet commemorates Tom Kettle there.

The fighting around this part of Flanders matched anything seen on the Somme for ferocity and it was particularly heavy during the first years of the war with advances and retreats under fire occurring on a regular basis. Many thousands died in this fighting even before the Somme offensive of 1916.

Tom Kettle was born in 1880, the seventh of twelve children of Andrew Kettle, a farmer and political activist who was one of the founders of the Land League and a strong supporter of Parnell. The family was comfortably off and Tom went first to O'Connell's Schools and then to Clongowes Wood College. He was a bright student and studied at University College Dublin, becoming friends with the likes of James Joyce and Oliver St John Gogarty. He later became Professor of Economics at UCD.

His political career began with a campaign against the Boer War (1899-1902) and his potential was spotted by the leader of the Irish Party, John Redmond. Although his views on issues like women's rights and education were regarded as very liberal he was chosen as the party candidate in East Tyrone in 1906 and was elected to the House of Commons at the age of twenty-six.

Kettle provided a great contrast to the aging conservative men who dominated the Irish Party. He became a star and was in great demand as a speaker and writer. An engaging and gregarious personality, he developed a fondness for drink that would become a problem as years went by. In 1909 he married Mary Sheehy, a fellow UCD graduate and suffragist, daughter of the Irish Party MP, David Sheehy, and sister of Hanna Sheehy Skeffington. Unlike other middle-class nationalists, Kettle had sympathy with the strikers during the Dublin Lockout of 1913 and wrote extensively about the appalling conditions of the Dublin poor.

Kettle joined the Irish Volunteers in 1913 and was in Belgium buying guns when the war broke out. He was horrified by the German atrocities he witnessed and wrote about them for the *Daily News*. His passionate feelings about Belgium's cause prompted him to back John Redmond's support for the British war effort, which Redmond stated in a speech in Woodenbridge, County Wicklow, on 20 September 1915. He joined the army, remarking, during one controversy: 'It is a confession to make and I make it. I care for liberty more than I care for Ireland.' He also thought that the involvement of National Volunteers (the name adopted by the majority of the Irish Volunteers who supported Redmond) and Ulster Volunteers as comrades in the war would prevent partition in the aftermath of the conflict. He was at the front when he heard about the Easter Rising of 1916 and in response to it he wrote: 'In the name and by the seal of the blood given in the last two years, I ask for colonial Home Rule for Ireland...and I ask for the immediate withdrawal of martial law in Ireland and an amnesty for all Sinn Féin prisoners.'

Conditions in the trenches quickly ruined Kettle's health but he refused to leave the Dublin Fusiliers for a safe job behind the lines. 'I have had two chances of leaving them, one on sick leave and the other to take a staff job. I have chosen to stay with my comrades. I am calm and happy and desperately anxious to live.'

Tom Kettle wrote a much-anthologised sonnet to his infant daughter Betty, whom he had never seen, a few days before he died. The poem captures the idealism of his sacrifice and that of his comrades in the 16th Irish Division. On 9 September 1916 Kettle was struck by a German bullet and died.

The Round Tower that forms part of the memorial to the Irish dead in Messines, Flanders

SO HERE, WHILE THE MAD GUNS
CURSE OVERHEAD,

AND TIRED MEN SIGH WITH MUD
FOR COUCH AND FLOOR,

KNOW THAT WE FOOLS, NOW WITH
THE FOOLISH DEAD,

DIED NOT FOR FLAG, NOR KING,
NOR EMPEROR,

BUT FOR A DREAM, BORN
IN A HERDMAN'S SHED,

AND FOR THE SECRET SCRIPTURE
OF THE POOR.

TOM KETTLE
9TH ROYAL DUBLIN FUSILIERS

The stone tablet commemorating Tom Kettle in Messines, Flanders
'But for a dream, born in a herdsman's shed,
And for the Secret Scripture of the poor.'

To My Daughter Betty, the Gift of God

(In the field, before Guillemot, Somme, 4 September 1916)

Tom Kettle

In wiser days, my darling rosebud, blown
To beauty proud as was your mother's prime –
In that desired, delayed, incredible time,
You'll ask why I abandoned you, my own,
And the dear breast that was your baby's throne,
To dice with death, and, oh! They'll give you rhyme,
And reason; one will call the thing sublime,
And one decry it in a knowing tone.
So here, while the mad guns curse overhead,
And tired men sigh, with mud for couch and floor,
Know that we fools, now with the foolish dead,
Died not for flag, nor king, nor emperor,
But for a dream, born in a herdsman's shed,
And for the Secret Scripture of the poor.

Crest of the Dublin Fusiliers, the regiment in which Tom Kettle served

John McCrae

John McCrae was born in Ontario in 1871, and qualified in medicine in Toronto in 1898. He enlisted in the British army when the Boer War began in 1899 and served with the artillery. From 1901 to 1914, he practised as a doctor in Canada and in England. He enlisted within the first few weeks of the outbreak of the First World War and was sent overseas in September 1914, again with the Canadian Field Artillery.

Whilst stationed in Essex Farm, in May 1915, during the second battle of Ypres, he was moved to write his famous poem 'In Flanders Fields', after one of his friends, Alexis Helmer, was killed by an exploding shell. McCrae was asked to conduct the burial service because the chaplain was on duty elsewhere and, seeing the poppies blowing around the graves, created the best-known image of this poem – and of the First World War as a whole. 'In Flanders Fields' was published for the first time in *Punch* on 8 December 1915 and has since come to encapsulate in the public imagination the sacrifice of those who fought. Alex Helmer's grave cannot be found in Essex Farm cemetery as it was lost later on in the war, and his name is commemorated among the 58,000 soldiers named on the Menin Gate.

Lieutenant Colonel John McCrae died of pneumonia on 28 January 1918 and was buried with full military honours in Wimereux Cemetery near Boulogne.

In Flanders Fields

John McCrae

In Flanders fields the poppies blow,
Between the crosses, row on row,
That mark our place; and in the sky,
The larks, still bravely singing, fly,
Scarce heard amid the guns below.

We are the Dead. Short days ago,
We lived, felt dawn, saw sunset glow,
Loved and were loved, and now we lie,
In Flanders fields.

Take up our quarrel with the foe:
To you from failing hands we throw,
The torch; be yours to hold it high.
If ye break faith with us who die,
We shall not sleep, though poppies grow,
In Flanders fields.

The clearing station near Essex Farm where John McCrae worked as a doctor

Music: Eric Bogle

Eric Bogle was born in Scotland in 1944, emigrated to Australia and worked as an accountant in Canberra before becoming a professional musician. He paid a holiday visit with his wife to some of the First World War graveyards in France and Flanders. As a result of this visit, Bogle wrote a wonderfully evocative song called 'No Man's Land', better known in Ireland as 'The Green Fields of France'. This part of Flanders, around the town of Ypres, with its pleasant and inviting landscape, is dotted with small and not so small memorials and graveyards. Tyne Cot is the location of one of the largest Commonwealth graveyards. Tyne Cot Cemetery is what is known as a concentration cemetery, as many of those interred there were moved from smaller cemeteries as the war progressed. It contains the bodies of some 12,000 men, although more than 8,000 were never identified.

Tyne Cot Cemetery derives from 'Tyne Cottage', the name the Northumberland Fusiliers gave to a barn near a level crossing on the road between Passchendaele and Broodseinde Ridge.

In Eric Bogle's song, Willie McBride's gravestone says he was nineteen years old when he died in 1916. According to the Commonwealth War Graves Commission, there were eight soldiers named 'William McBride' and a further six listed as 'W. McBride', who died in France or Belgium during the First World War, but none matches the soldier in the song. Two William McBrides and one W. McBride died in 1916 but one is commemorated on the Thiepval Memorial on the Somme and has no gravestone. The other two are buried in Authuille British Cemetery but one was aged twenty-one and the age of the other is unknown. All three were from Irish regiments. Three William McBrides fell in 1916; two were members of an Irish regiment, the Royal Inniskilling Fusiliers, and died in more or less in the same spot during the Battle of the Somme. One was twenty-one, the other nineteen years old.

A nineteen-year-old Private William McBride is buried in Authuille Cemetery, near Albert and Beaumont-Hamel, where the Inniskilling Fusiliers fought as part of the 29th Division.

The Green Fields of France

Eric Bogle

Well, how do you do, Private William McBride,
Do you mind if I sit down here by your graveside?
And rest for a while in the warm summer sun,
I've been walking all day and I'm nearly done.
And I see by your gravestone you were only nineteen,
When you joined the glorious fallen in 1916,
Well, I hope you died quick and I hope you died clean,
Or, Willie McBride, was it slow and obscene?

Chorus
Did they beat the drum slowly, did the play the pipes lowly?
Did the rifles fire o'er you as they lowered you down?
Did the bugles sound 'The Last Post' in chorus?
Did the pipes play 'The Flowers of the Forest'?

And did you leave a wife or a sweetheart behind?
In some loyal heart is your memory enshrined?
And, though you died back in 1916,
To that loyal heart are you forever nineteen?
Or are you a stranger without even a name,
Forever enshrined behind some glass pane,
In an old photograph, torn and tattered and stained,
And fading to yellow in a brown leather frame?

The sun's shining down on these green fields of France;
The warm wind blows gently and the red poppies dance.
The trenches have vanished long under the plough;
No gas and no barbed wire, no guns firing now.
But here in this graveyard that's still no man's land,
The countless white crosses in mute witness stand,
To man's blind indifference to his fellow man,
And a whole generation who were butchered and damned.

And I can't help but wonder, now Willie McBride,
Do all those who lie here know why they died?
Did you really believe them when they told you 'the cause'?
Did you really believe that this war would end wars?
Well, the suffering, the sorrow, the glory, the shame,
The killing, the dying, it was all done in vain,
For Willie McBride, it all happened again,
And again, and again, and again, and again.

The Allied Cemetery at Tynecot

What Did You Do in the War, Granny?

The involvement of women in the war effort both at home and at the front has been consistently underestimated and often forgotten. Married women, perhaps with young families of their own, would have had a difficult time making ends meet during the tough economic times that existed in 1914. They would have waged their own war on deprivation and hunger during the years of conflict. But they endured the hardship quietly and without any accolade or citation. In First World War Dublin many members of the fairer sex worked for the Irish soldiers in France and other battle zones. The women of the Dublin Unionist Club decided to collect newspapers, magazines and books to dispatch to the men in the trenches. The Irish Sisters of Charity took to making shirts for the British army in their convent in Baldoyle, County Dublin. There was nothing charitable about this work – it was a business arrangement. At the end of the war, when there was no more need for army shirts, the nuns turned their skills to crochet work, knitwear and the manufacture of silk garments.

The majority of the young ladies who volunteered for service were in their late teens to mid-twenties. Some of them, like Marie Martin (1892-1975) and Rosemary Savage, served near the front as VADs (members of the Voluntary Aid Detachment). Others, like Monica Roberts, served the cause at home. Marie Martin served as a volunteer in Malta, where she tended many of the Gallipoli wounded, before she left for a field hospital in France. She nursed the wounded all through the Somme campaign. Rosemary Savage lived in Cushendall, County Antrim, where she and her mother ran fundraising events in aid of the comfort fund for the 13th Royal Irish Rifles. Monica Roberts and a friend used to give song recitals in the parish halls of south County Dublin in order to raise money to buy sweets, cigarettes and gloves to send as comfort parcels to soldiers of the Dublin Fusiliers in France. Monica Roberts wrote to some of the men who were around her own age, hoping to alleviate their loneliness.

Sophia Violet Barrett was born in Ballintava, near Dunmore in County Galway. Known as 'Violet' to her family, she joined the Carrickmines and Kingstown branch of the VAD and volunteered for service. She had been staying with her aunt Marcella, the wife of William Wilson of Carrickmines House, Foxrock, and initially she was posted to Monkstown Auxiliary Hospital in County Dublin. This large private house had been donated for use as an officer's hospital. Later she was sent to Leeds northern hospital and then on to France, where she served in both Rouen and Abbeville. She was mentioned in dispatches during Christmas of 1917, which entitled her to wear two stripes on her nurse's uniform. She finished her stint at the front near Abbeville, nursing German prisoners, then returned to Foxrock.

Sophia Violet Barrett was killed while returning to the front from leave aboard the RMS *Leinster*, which was torpedoed just outside Dublin Bay on 10 October 1918, a month before the war ended. Her body was recovered and interred in Kilternan cemetery and after the war a silver chalice was donated in her honour to Tully Church, Foxrock, where it is used to this day.

By the end of the war, the Irish branches of the British Red Cross Society and the St John's Ambulance Brigade had established eighty-three women's VAD units, with 2927 members, mostly in Dublin. By the end of May 1914 the Ulster VAD had 3520 members throughout the province.

Marie Martin returned from the war and, after serving as a lay missionary in Nigeria, set up the Medical Missionaries of Mary in 1937. Monica Roberts married and reared a family; she died in 1974. Rosemary Savage married an Irish soldier in India and came home to live in Bandon. She died in 1983, having reached the great age of 90.

'On a quiet street where old ghosts meet': Patrick Kavanagh's

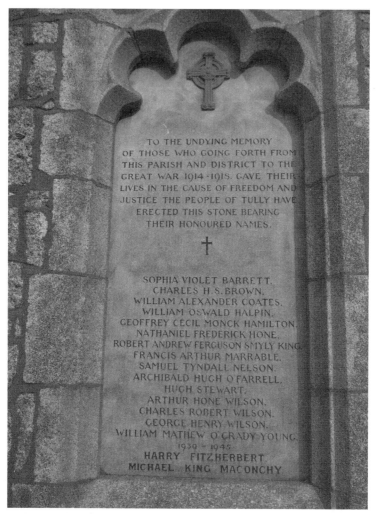

TO THE UNDYING MEMORY
OF THOSE WHO GOING FORTH FROM
THIS PARISH AND DISTRICT TO THE
GREAT WAR 1914-1918 GAVE THEIR
LIVES IN THE CAUSE OF FREEDOM AND
JUSTICE THE PEOPLE OF TULLY HAVE
ERECTED THIS STONE BEARING
THEIR HONOURED NAMES.

†

SOPHIA VIOLET BARRETT,
CHARLES H.S. BROWN,
WILLIAM ALEXANDER COATES,
WILLIAM OSWALD HALPIN,
GEOFFREY CECIL MONCK HAMILTON,
NATHANIEL FREDERICK HONE,
ROBERT ANDREW FERGUSON SMYLY KING,
FRANCIS ARTHUR MARRABLE,
SAMUEL TYNDALL NELSON,
ARCHIBALD HUGH O'FARRELL,
HUGH STEWART,
ARTHUR HONE WILSON,
CHARLES ROBERT WILSON,
GEORGE HENRY WILSON,
WILLIAM MATHEW O'GRADY YOUNG,
1939-1945
HARRY FITZHERBERT
MICHAEL KING MACONCHY

A plaque in Tully Church, Foxroxk, commemorates Violet Barrett, who lost her life when the RMS Leinster *was torpedoed and sank on 10 October 1918*

line from 'Raglan Road' comes to mind as I cross Blackhorse Avenue, not always a quiet street, from the Phoenix Park. At this early hour, I enter the leafy oasis that is Grangegorman Military Cemetery. The cemetery dates back to 1786 and contains the remains of men who served in British forces and their families. The cemetery has a mix of normal headstones and a number of the more traditional flat, military stones and it is interesting to see just how many different regiments are listed here. It's clear that Irishmen enlisting in the British forces enlisted not only in Irish regiments but across the whole range of regiments.

What caught my eye, however, was the number of headstones with the date of 10 October 1918. I realised that here lay soldiers who were killed in the sinking of the RMS *Leinster* on that fateful night. Any soldier during a war would have expected to come under fire and understood that his life was at risk but the soldiers on this ship must have felt that they were relatively safe as they were so close to home.

Grangegorman Military Cemetery, Dublin

When the ship was torpedoed, it sank quickly with five hundred casualties: men, women and children. A poignant aspect of this story was the loss of twenty post office workers who were working as sorters on the ship that night. For security reasons they were sorting in a locked cage and they were unable to get out. The Holyhead to Kingstown mail boat, the RMS *Leinster*, belonged to the City of Dublin Steam Packet Company and carried passengers and mail between Ireland and Wales. During the conflict the Irish Sea was the scene of much U-boat activity and the Germans had made several attempts to sink boats of the mail service before this. The mail boats were relatively fast vessels and relied on speed rather than convoy protection to carry them safely across the Irish Sea.

The *Leinster* was attacked by the German submarine UB123 off the Kish Bank. It was carrying more than seven hundred passengers, of whom about three hundred would have been soldiers bound for England and the Continent. The ship was torpedoed twice, the second strike three minutes after the first. The first torpedo struck the post office quarters, killing all but one of the post office staff. In total only two hundred-and-fifty-six people were rescued, most of the survivors being taken to hospital in Kingstown (now Dún Laoghaire).

Women, like men, were divided in their reactions to war, with some championing the cause and others opposing it. The National Union of Women's Suffrage Societies in Britain put political activity on hold for the duration of the war, although in 1915 there were public demonstrations demanding that women be given a 'right to serve'. Emmeline Pankurst (1858-1928) and her daughter Christabel 1880-1958), the most famous suffragists, turned to recruiting soldiers for the war effort. On the other hand, Christabel's sister Sylvia (1882-1960) remained opposed to the war, as did other suffragists; in Germany, the socialist thinker and later revolutionary Rosa Luxembourg was imprisoned for much of the war because of her opposition to it.

In the United States, President Woodrow Wilson was won over to the suffragists' side in part because of the bravery of women serving on the front and the abilities they showed themselves to have as they replaced men in offices and factories. In September 1918 Wilson addressed the Senate, urging that it follow the House in passing the 19th Amendment to allow women to vote, in recognition of the contributions made by American women in the war: 'Are we alone to ask and take the utmost that our women can give, service and sacrifice of every kind, and still say we do not see what title that gives them to stand by our sides in the guidance of the affairs of their nations and ours? We have made partners of the women in this war; shall we admit them only to a partnership of suffering and sacrifice and toil and not to a partnership of privilege and right?'

The use of women in propaganda was established early in the war, when posters and later cinema were used to promote a vision of the war as one where soldiers defended women, as well as children and their homeland. The British and French response to the alleged German 'Rape of Belgium', when reports of German atrocities were highlighted, was to cast Belgian women in the role of defenceless victims. One poster used in Ireland featured a women standing with a rifle in front of a burning Belgium.

Women were used on recruiting posters throughout the war, applying moral and family/social pressure on men to join up or else be scorned. This publicity, along with Britain's 'white feather' campaigns, in which women were encouraged to give white feathers to men who were not in uniform as symbols of cowardice, as well as women's role as recruiters for the armed forces, was designed to 'persuade' men into the armed forces. Furthermore, some posters presented young and sexually attractive women as rewards for soldiers.

But it wasn't all cakes and ale. This was war after all and war is a poor respecter of class and gender. Many women and children in the civilian population lost their lives during the war, not only in the occupied areas in France and Belgium but in bombing raids in London and elsewhere.

The Rose of No Man's Land

Jack Caddigan

I've seen some beautiful flowers,
Grow in my garden fair,
I've spent some wonderful hours,
Lost in their fragrance rare.
But I have found another,
Wondrous beyond compare.

There's a rose that grows on no man's land,
And it's wonderful to see;
Though its place is there it will live for me,
In my garden of memories.

It's the one red rose the soldier knows,
It's the work of the Master's hand,
It's the sweet word from the Red Cross nurse,
She's the rose of no man's land.

If You Were the only Boche in the World

Anon

Trench version of 'If You Were the Only Girl in the World' (1916)

If you were the only Boche in the trench,
And I had the only bomb,
Nothing else would matter in the world today,
I would blow you in to eternity.
Chamber of Horrors, just made for two,
With nothing to spoil our fun;
There would be such a heap of things to do,
I should get your rifle and bayonet too,
If you were the only Boche in the trench,
And I had the only gun.

One of a network of Canadian trenches still visible today
near Sanctuary Wood (Hill 62) in Flanders

7

Gallipoli and the Dardanelles

St Audeon's, High Street, is Dublin's earliest surviving medieval church. The 12th-century tower is believed to be the oldest in Ireland, and its three bells date from 1423. Although High Street was one of Dublin's most important medieval streets, by the time the twentieth century had begun it was a poor neighbourhood in the very heart of Dublin's tenements. Places like 'Cut Purse Row' and 'Carnal Way' were close by and because of the local food market (the Cornmarket) it was a bustling area.

Patrick Walsh lived in High Street. In 1915 he was twenty-eight, married to Katy and the father of two children, a daughter, Elizabeth, and a son, Patrick. He was working as a labourer in Boland's Mills on Grand Canal Street to support his young family, when tragedy struck and his wife died in childbirth. The loss of his wife and their newborn, his third child, must have been a crushing blow in what would otherwise have been a contented, if not carefree, existence.

As a working man in Bolands Mills, Patrick was probably better off than most of his working-class comrades living in the High Street tenements. (He was earning twenty-eight shillings a week.) It's hard to understand why exactly he would have chosen the path to war that he took. After the lockout of 1913, conditions were very tough on families in inner-city Dublin but Patrick would have considered himself one of the lucky ones to be working at all. Clearly there were many men who had no work and saw the army simply as a financial means to an end. Other young men were motivated by the idea of some form of travel or adventure. They hoped the army would provide them with a great chance to 'see the world'.

Whatever the reason, Patrick entrusted the care of his young son and daughter to his mother-in-law and enlisted in the Dublin Fusiliers. They never saw him again, and when the letter from the British War Office arrived to tell them that he had been killed in action on 17 September 1915, they presumed he had been in France. In fact he was killed in Suvla Bay in Gallipoli, many miles from home.

To this day the feelings of Patrick's grandchild about his loss is tinged with anger: anger at the waste of his young life, a life that held so much potential for a family struggling to make ends meet and achieve some kind of happiness. It is clear to me that the reluctance of war veterans to speak openly, or even in private, about the conditions they had to endure in the trenches has had a lasting effect on those left behind. It is hard for those who did not experience it to understand what the soldiers suffered. But how could you speak about these conditions without having to endure the horrors all over again in your mind?

The grave of Patrick Walsh in Greenhill Cemetery, near Suvla Bay

Gallipoli is a wonderful place, as the line in the song relates, but during the summer of 1915 when British troops clung on to the small areas of ground they had gained from the Turks, the heat was intense. Water had to be rationed. Diseases such as dysentery were rampant and dehydration was a constant problem. With winter came a biting wind and snow. The intense cold and damp caused terrible trench foot and frostbite. Men died in horrible circumstances which had little to do with being shot by the enemy. Families who had to bear the loss of their loved ones did not always see the gallant side of war; nor did they think of the dead as heroes.

Two Irish brothers, Jack and George Duggan, died in Gallipoli on the same day, 16 August 1915, and a third brother, George Chester wrote a poem to their memory, the poem that gave this book its title. The brothers had sailed from Dublin's North Wall, Jack as a lieutenant in the 5th Royal Irish Regiment and George as a captain in the Royal Irish Fusiliers.

Patrick Walsh landed with his regiment in Suvla Bay on the Aegean side of the Gallipoli peninsula in May 1915. Although there was stalemate from the point of view of movement or territorial gain across this area, the fighting was fierce, with attack and counter-attack taking the lives of almost 50,000 young men by the time the British forces were withdrawn just after Christmas 1915. The first British troops had landed near Hellespoint on a beach designated 'Y' beach. In the disarray of a night time landing with poor communications they did not navigate accurately and went somewhat astray, landing about a mile away from their target.

French troops landed successfully on the Asian side, close to where the Tusan Hotel stands today, but were quickly withdrawn to help the British and Australian forces who were facing dogged resistance. The Irish landed further north on 'V' beach, where they met strong resistance, and in Suvla where they initially got ashore with no resistance. (Again, due to poor communications they failed to push forward and take the high ground, such as it was, ahead of them. They later paid heavily for this mistake.)

The grave of an Irish soldier 'believed to be buried' in Gallipoli

*Graves in Anzac Cove. The hills in the background held
the Turkish machine gun emplacements.*

I cannot describe the feeling of standing in some of the cemeteries on the Gallipoli peninsula. To a large extent time has stood still here and the cemeteries are in some of the most beautiful and idyllic places you could ever hope to find. But the story they tell is a complete contradiction. Dead young men, some not even found but 'believed to be here', azure sea quietly rippling on to a beach, where the white sand is almost as bright as the white crosses set in little lines, 'in mute witness', to mark the final resting place of a generation of young soldiers lost in battle. When you look from Suvla Bay across to the south you can see two hills not too far away. One is quite green – this is Chocolate Hill – and the other is definitely brown. This is Greenhill, where Patrick Walsh is buried with his comrades. (Obviously these hills have changed in colour over time.) This is as far as they made it, maybe a mile from the salt flats that surround Suvla Bay.

More recently the Germans opposed the British across another imaginary line, a line struck across the dining room of the Tusan Hotel in Çanakkale, Turkey. Today, Çanakkale is a small bustling town on the Asian side of the long stretch of water known as the Dardanelles, the strait that separates Europe and Asia. Herr Doctor Baum's archaeological group was facing the British specialist touring party visiting the Gallipoli war sites. The German party had just returned from the ancient ruins of the city of Troy, situated to the south. They were ebullient and the noise level soared. Happily, on this occasion, there were no casualties and the room was buzzing with friendly chatter in both German and English. Almost a hundred years ago, during the Gallipoli campaign in 1915, when these two nations opposed each other – the Germans allied with the Turkish forces – only a few miles away to the east, the distance between them was sometimes no more than it is now, across this crowded room on this enchanting evening. The view from the Tusan Hotel's dining room across the Dardanelles towards the Gallipoli peninsula was breathtaking and, on a recent trip back to this part of Turkey, I was touched by the splendour of colours in the sunset over one of the most beautiful and untouched war sites.

The entire Gallipoli peninsula has been designated a national park and conservation area by the Turkish government, in deference to the men who bravely fought and died here. Virtually nothing has changed in the last hundred years and all development has been stopped and in some cases even reversed to maintain the peninsula in as close to its original form as possible. The dead have been interred in many small cemeteries dotted around the area. Even up to the early 1960s the fields and ditches were yielding up the remains of fallen soldiers. Walking through some of the rugged landscape today, over areas where intense battles were fought, you may discover items of armour that have been buried. In March 2010 President Mary McAleese unveiled a commemorative plaque to the Irish dead in Greenhill cemetery.

Greenhill Cemetery, where President Mary McAleese unveiled a plaque in 2010

During the Gallipoli campaign, which lasted only two hundred and fifty days, some one thousand casualties occurred on each side every day. In some places the trenches were no more than eight metres apart and the longest part of the front line stretched for only six kilometres. This meant that every square metre of front line could have up to four bodies lying in it at any time. The conditions that the men endured while fighting here – among the wild flowers that bloomed as the campaign began in early spring 1915 – must have been horrendous.

Winston Churchill, First Lord of the Admiralty at the beginning the war (as he was at the beginning of the Second World War), believed that the Bosphorus, the strait between Asia and Europe, could be taken by using just the British navy's considerable power. To be fair, the feat had been accomplished a century before by Admiral Duckworth in the *Royal George;* however, the second attempt by Vice-Admiral Sir John de Robeck on 18 March 1915 failed miserably, with the loss of three battleships. It was a simple task for soldiers of the German and Turkish alliance to mine the straits and train large guns to cover this narrow stretch of coastline.

Today, as in 1915, the Dardanelles are among the busiest waterways in the world and when they were blockaded during the war more than 30 per cent of the world's shipping fleet was confined in the straits.

After the failure of the naval campaign the Gallipoli landings were the next plank of Churchill's strategy. Lord Allenbrook, who was appointed as Winston Churchill's Commander Imperial General Staff (CIGS) at an early stage of the war, kept a very interesting, detailed diary of his time as CIGS. Of Winston Churchill he wrote that he was a person who could have more than twenty strategic ideas every day, at least nineteen of which were complete rubbish and perhaps one that was genius. It was part of Allenbrook's job to keep track of these ideas and make the most of them as they issued from the great man. This was no easy task, as Churchill had a habit of discussing the ideas with many of the different players involved in a situation and then playing one off the others until he got his way or the idea lost traction and moved on. Churchill's strategy of forcing the Dardanelles was a real disaster during the First World War.

So began the Gallipoli campaign, with landings at a number of points beginning with Cape Helles on 25 April 1915. On the European side the land is quite rugged in places, with low hills divided by jagged, rocky valleys and outcrops, dropping down to small coves and beaches. Only 3 per cent of present-day Turkey lies in Europe, and this peninsula is most of it. The outcrops and ridges gave a great advantage to the Turkish troops who held the high ground when the first British and untested Anzac (Australian and New Zealand Army Corps) soldiers arrived.

When Churchill's great plan was rolled out, Mustapha Kemal Ataturk was a captain in the Turkish army, stationed in Boghali, close to the Dardanelles. Kemal first arrived at Chunuk Bar after a difficult march with his troops from Baghali, They did not know the area well themselves and had to resort to a map and Kemal's small compass to find their way. Kemal rested his men and moved forward himself to see what was happening, only to meet some Turkish soldiers in full retreat from the advancing Australians.

It appears that the young captain had the good sense to see that the heights of Chunuk Bar held the key to the peninsula. Had the Anzac forces successfully taken and held it in this early phase of the campaign it is likely that there would have been a different outcome entirely. The wily young captain managed to stop his fleeing troops and when they complained that they had no ammunition he told them to fix bayonets and lie flat on the ground. The Australians also decided to take cover, fearing a much bigger opposing force. This hesitation allowed Kemal to send for reinforcements and dig in. The landing troops did not manage to achieve any of their primary objectives in the first days' fighting and the campaign disintegrated into a bloody struggle for virtually every inch of ground over the next nine months, until eventually the British forces were evacuated by sea to Cyprus.

Kemal fought with tremendous bravery and skill throughout the Gallipoli campaign but his attributes as a leader of men really became evident after the war when Turkey, on the losing side, was being pushed into accepting harsh reparations, including the loss of some islands to Greece. Ataturk became prime minister of Turkey and is known as the father of the modern Turkish state.

It occurred to me when I visited Çanakkale and Istanbul that the Turks, who are friendly and polite, seem to have a very similar outlook on life to the Irish. This attitude towards foreigners is a scarce commodity in any modern city, let alone one like Istanbul, that has nearly fifteen million inhabitants.

After the débâcle at Gallipoli, Churchill was replaced as First Lord of the Admiralty.

Music

The Anzac troops had a particularly difficult baptism of fire when they arrived at Anzac Cove, as it is now known. It is overlooked by a scarp between two low hills and this provided perfect cover or the Turkish machine guns when the Australians landed in early May 1915. Many songs have been written about the Anzac landings, with titles such as 'At the Call of Britannia, Australia Faced the Foe'. 'Brave Australians 'and 'The Boys of the Dardanelles'.

'Old Gallipoli's a Wonderful Place' is a trench song. The melody is that of 'The Mountains of Mourne' by Percy French (1854-1920), already used by Thomas Moore (1779–1852) for his song 'Bendemeer's Stream'. Trench songs were normally devised by the troops, who used a well-known melody and wrote words to suit the situation. There are many examples of these songs, which were sometimes printed in the trench newspapers available from time to time for the troops. They might be specific to an area as in 'old Gallipoli', but more often than not the same songs were sung by troops in different combat zones.

'Waltzing Matilda' is Australia's most widely known bush ballad, and is regarded as 'the unofficial national anthem of Australia'. The title is Australian slang for travelling on foot with

The graveyard at Anzac Cove, Gallipoli, where Anzac troops landed on 25 April 1915, more than a mile away from the proposed landing site at Gaba Tebe beach. Nearby a monument displays the words of Ataturk:
'Those heroes that shed their blood and lost their lives. You are living in the soil of a friendly country, therefore rest in peace. There is no difference between the Johnnies and Mehmets to us where they lie side by side here in this country of ours... You the mothers who sent their sons from far away countries wipe away your tears. Your sons are now lying in our bosom and are in peace. After having lost their lives on this land they have become our sons as well.'

one's goods in a 'matilda' or bag slung over one's shoulder. It's the story of a worker, or swagman, making tea at his bush camp and 'liberating' a sheep to eat. The original lyrics were written in 1895 by the poet and nationalist Banjo Paterson and the song published as sheet music in 1903. Eric Bogle used 'Waltzing Matilda' as the starting point for a song in memory of the Anzacs who landed and fought at Gallipoli and the 50,000 Australian dead). The title is 'And the Band Played Waltzing Matilda'.

Alec Campbell, the last known survivor of the ANZAC forces who landed in Gallipoli died on 16 May 2002 at the age of a hundred and three. Campbell enlisted at sixteen and served in Gallipoli in 1915. He led the ANZAC Day parade in Hobart, Tasmania, three weeks before his death.

At the Call of Britannia, Australia Faced the Foe

Arnold Rodda

At the call of Britannia,
Australia faced the foe,
Ready to die for the dear old flag,
Like their fathers long ago.
Glorious boys of Anzac,
Fearless, brave and true.
Have shown the German Kaiser,
What Australian lads can do'.

Old Gallipoli's a Wonderful Place

Anon

Oh, old Gallipoli's a wonderful place,
Where the boys in the trenches the foe have to face,
But they never grumble, they smile through it all,
Very soon they expect Achi Baba to fall.
At least when I asked them, that's what they told me,
In Constantinople quite soon we would be,
But if war lasts till Doomsday I think we'll still be,
Where old Gallipoli sweeps down to the sea.

We don't grow potatoes or barley or wheat,
So we're on the lookout for something to eat,
We're fed up with biscuits and bully and ham,
And we're sick of the sight of yon parapet jam.
Send out steak and onions and nice ham and eggs,
And a fine big fat chicken with five or six legs,
And a drink of the stuff that begins with a 'B',
Where old Gallipoli sweeps down to the sea.

And the Band Played Waltzing Matilda

Eric Bogle

When I was a young man I carried my pack,
And I lived the free life of a rover,
From the Murrays green basin to the dusty outback,
I waltzed my Matilda all over.
Then in nineteen fifteen my country said, 'Son,
It's time to stop rambling 'cause there's work to be done.'
So they gave me a tin hat and they gave me a gun,
And they sent me away to the war.

Chorus
And the band played Waltzing Matilda,
As we sailed away from the quay,
And amidst all the tears and the shouts and the cheers,
We sailed off to Gallipoli.

How well I remember that terrible day,
How the blood stained the sand and the water.
And how in that hell that they called Suvla Bay,
We were butchered like lambs at the slaughter.
Johnny Turk he was ready, he primed himself well,
He chased us with bullets, he rained us with shells,
And in five minutes flat he'd blown us all to hell,
Nearly blew us right back to Australia.

Chorus
But the band played Waltzing Matilda,
As we stopped to bury our slain,
We buried ours and the Turks buried theirs,
Then we started all over again.

Now those who were left, well, we tried to survive,
In a mad world of blood, death and fire,
And for ten weary weeks I kept myself alive,
But around me the corpses piled higher,
Then a big Turkish shell knocked me arse over tit,
And when I woke up in my hospital bed,
And saw what it had done, I wished I was dead,
Never knew there were worse things than dying.

Chorus
For no more I'll go waltzing Matilda,
All around the green bush far and near,
For to hump tent and pegs, a man needs two legs,
No more waltzing Matilda for me

So they collected the cripples, the wounded, the maimed,
And they shipped us back home to Australia,
The armless, the legless, the blind, the insane,
Those proud wounded heroes of Suvla.
And as our ship pulled into Circular Quay,
I looked at the place where my legs used to be,
And thanked Christ there was nobody waiting for me,
To grieve and to mourn and to pity,

Chorus
And the band played Waltzing Matilda,
As they carried us down the gangway,
But nobody cheered, they just stood and stared,
Then turned all their faces away.

And now every April I sit on my porch,
And I watch the parade pass before me,
And I see my old comrades, how proudly they march,
Reliving old dreams of past glory.
And the old men march slowly, all bent, stiff and sore,
The forgotten heroes from a forgotten war,

And the young people ask, 'What are they marching for?'
And I ask myself the same question.

Chorus
And the band plays Waltzing Matilda,
And the old men answer to the call,
But year after year their numbers get fewer,
Some day no one will march there at all.

Waltzing Matilda, Waltzing Matilda,
Who'll come a waltzing Matilda with me?
And their ghosts may be heard as you pass the billabong,
Who'll come-a-waltzing Matilda with me?

8

Many Young Men (and Not so Young)

'Many young men of twenty said goodbye.' The words of the evocative song from the play, *Many Young Men of Twenty* (1961) by John B Keane (1928-2002), especially in Johnny McEvoy's recording, are a tragic reminder of the loss of young men and boys, although Keane's play dealt not with war but with the mass emigration from Ireland that was a fact of life until the 1960s. In the First World War, although the young men went as individuals, the fought en masse and died en masse, faceless and in some instances nameless in death: the phrase 'Known unto God' appears on many gravestones in France and Belgium. However the more I read and research these faceless men the more their individuality emerges. They were young but with real hopes and dreams and often careers, families and a reason to live. Francis Ledwidge (1887-1917) was a published poet at the age of fourteen and had a mentor and patron in Lord Dunsany. No need for him to join the army to survive! Lawrence Kelly had a permanent and pensionable position at Arthur Guinness; Patrick Walsh worked in Boland's Mills. And so on.

The youngest casualty of the First World War was only fourteen when he was killed in Flanders. John Condon, the boy soldier from Waterford, trained for military service in the army barracks in Clonmel, County Tipperary, after he fooled a British army recruiting officer into believing he was eighteen years of age.

John Condon's family discovered he was in Belgium only when the British army wrote to them after he went missing in action on 24 May 1915. Condon's father informed the military authorities of his son's real age and the military records in London were amended. Ten years would pass before John

Condon's body was discovered by a farmer and his remains finally laid to rest in Poelcapelle cemetery near Ypres.

By contrast, the man buried beside him, a Private T. Carthy, also from Waterford, was one of the oldest killed in action, at the age of forty-seven. It is often difficult to understand why particular individuals went to war. Perhaps it was as Francis Ledwidge had suggested: that they did not want other men to

have to fight for freedoms that they would later enjoy.

Ledwidge himself, sometimes known as the 'poet of the black-birds' was a nationalist but nevertheless signed up in October 1914 and served in Gallipoli and Serbia. He seemed to believe that by fighting for the British he was furthering the cause of Irish independence and it is also thought that he had recently been disappointed in love. Ledwidge seems to have fitted well

into army life and rapidly achieved promotion to lance corporal. In 1915, he saw action in Suvla Bay, where he suffered severe rheumatism. Later his company sustained huge losses. While still on active service in Gallipoli he received the news that his collection, *Songs of the Field*, had been published and had been well received by the press. Ledwidge was recovering from wounds in hospital in Manchester when he heard the news of the 1916 Rising. He wrote his most famous poem in response to the death of Thomas MacDonagh, one of the executed leaders.

Francis Ledwidge was killed by a shell on 31 July 1917 when a group from the 1st Battalion of the Royal Inniskillen Fusiliers of which he was a member was repairing the road to Pilkem near the village of Boezinghe, north-west of Ypres. This was in preparation for the third battle of Passchendaele. The group of soldiers was drinking tea when they were hit. The brigade chaplain, Father Devas, who knew Ledwidge well, identified him and recorded 'Ledwidge killed, blown to bits'. Lawrence Kelly died nearby on the same day.

Frances Ledwidge was just a few weeks short of his thirtieth birthday when he died. He was buried at Carrefour de Rose, and later reinterred in the nearby Artillery Wood Military Cemetery, Boezinghe, where the Welsh poet Hedd Wyn, killed on the same day, is also buried.

Of course not all the individuals serving in the British Army during the war were talented poets or artists. Many were simple but tough men, able to endure the hardships of trench warfare. We have heard a lot recently about Tom Crean, the Antarctic explorer from Annascaul in County Kerry. Crean was one such tough individual, capable of enduring what the Antarctic had to throw at him. He sailed for Antarctica with Scott on the day war broke out in 1914. They had to have special permission from the king to continue with the exploration, given the situation at home. Several men of the expedition, who had been rescued by the indomitable Crean, returned to England and immediately enlisted. Most were subsequently killed on the Somme.

Another man of great endurance was John Moyney from

The grave of Francis Ledwidge in Artillery Wood Military Cemetery

On this spot was killed
the Irish poet and soldier

Op deze plek sneuvelde
de Ierse dichter-soldaat

FRANCIS
LEDWIDGE

* Slane 19 august 1887 / + Boezinge 31 july 1917

He shall not hear
the bittern cry
in the wild sky,
where he is lain

Hij zal de roerdomp
niet horen roepen
in de wilde lucht,
waar hij ligt

Monument to Francis Ledwidge in Artillery Wood Military Cemetery

Rathdowney in County Laois. Moyney was twenty-two years old and a lance-sergeant in the 2nd Battalion, Irish Guards, when he was awarded the Victoria Cross (VC). There are not many Irish recipients of the Victoria Cross, the highest award that can be awarded to British and Commonwealth forces for gallantry in the face of the enemy – and even fewer who lived to receive the decoration in person.

On 12 September 1917, just north of Broembeek, in Flanders, Lance-Sergeant Moyney was in command of fifteen men forming two advance posts. Surrounded by the enemy, he held his post for ninety-six hours, with no water and very little food. On the fifth day, the enemy advanced to try to dislodge him; he attacked them with bombs, while also using his Lewis gun to great effect. Finding himself surrounded, he led his men in a charge through the enemy and reached a stream, where he and a private, Private Thomas Woodcock (also awarded the Victoria Cross), covered his party while they crossed unscathed, before crossing themselves under a shower of bullets.

Moyney later achieved the rank of sergeant but was demoted after a court martial for being drunk and disorderly. He died in Roscrea, County Tipperary, on 10 November 1980, at the age of eighty-five, and, although he never spoke much about his exploits, he did complain to officialdom after the war that his pension was not sufficient to live on.

His son James served in the British army during the Second World War. Having fought his way through north Africa, he was captured in Anzio in Italy and saw out the rest of the war in a German POW camp. James also died in his eighty-fifth year.

Thomas Woodcock was born in Wigan, Lancashire, in 1888. A private at the time he was awarded the Victoria Cross, he was later promoted to corporal. He was killed in action on 27 March 1918 and is buried at Douchy-les-Ayette British Cemetery near Arras.

John Moyney's Victoria Cross is displayed at the Irish Guards Regimental Headquarters in London.

The Irish Guards were raised as a regiment in 1900 by order

John Moyney, who was awarded the Victoria Cross for gallantry in 1917

John Moyney's comrade in arms, Thomas Woodcok, who was also awarded the Victoria Cross in 1917

of Queen Victoria, in honour of the brave Irishmen who fought in the British army during the two Boer wars, as a mark of the Crown's appreciation of their exceptional gallantry at the Siege of Ladysmith (1899-1900), during the Second Boer War. During the battles at Ladysmith and Bloemfontein Irishmen of the Inniskilling Fusiliers, the Dublin Fusiliers and the Connaught Rangers, in particular, had distinguished themselves by their bravery and, as there were already regiments of Scots Guards and English Guards, it was decided that a regiment of Irish Guards should be created.

Sergeant-Major Martin Doyle (1891-1940) of the Munster Fusiliers was awarded a Victoria Cross for the act of gallantry described by this citation: 'On 2 September 1918 at Reincourt, France, when command of the company fell on Company Sergeant-Major Doyle, all the officers having become casualties, he extricated a party of his men who were surrounded by the enemy, and carried back, under heavy fire, a wounded officer. Later he went forward under intense fire to the assistance of a tank and when an enemy machine-gun opened fire on the tank, making it impossible to get the wounded away, he captured it single-handed and took three prisoners. Subsequently when the enemy counter-attacked, he drove them back, taking many more prisoners.'

Like John Moyney, Martin Doyle survived the war and joined the Irish army after independence.

The grave of Martin Doyle in Grangegorman Military Cemetery, Dublin

Serving the Crown

Paul O'Brien

This morning the captain said,
It's time for the push,
So we climbed on the ladders,
And then came the rush.
Now we got twenty yards,
When the Hun opened fire,
And left all of my friends dead,
Or stuck hung on the wire.

Chorus
And I can still see her waving;
I can still hear the crowd.
When we sailed out for Flanders,
To be serving the Crown.

Now the captain's lying,
A few feet away,
He's sunk in the mud,
And covered in clay.
He wants me to help him,
He wants it to end,
But I'm keeping my head down,
Because it's starting again.

They promised we'd be home,
By Christmas at least,
The Hun would see sense,
And come begging for peace.
Just more of the lies,
And false promises made.
I don't need to dress up,
For this Easter parade.

Talbot House (Toc H) in Ypres as it looks today. During the war, as Every Man's Club, it was a place of refuge for officers and men. It was run by a chaplain, the Reverent Philip Clayton, and named for Gilbert Talbot, son of the Bishop of Winchester, who had been killed in 1915. Plays and revues and other items of entertainment were staged there for the war-weary troops. A notice was hung by the front door bearing the message: 'All rank abandon, ye who enter here.'

Sign at the Every Man's Club, Talbot House, Ypres

9

The Yanks are Coming

As was the case in the Second World War, the arrival of the Americans into the First World War was to prove decisive. The sheer weight of numbers in men and machinery seemed to make a lasting difference between the two sides and increasingly it became obvious to the German High Command that the situation of the country's army was becoming more and more impossible.

In April 1915, President Woodrow Wilson declared that he would keep America out of the war. Germany's submarine warfare against Britain intensified: the Cunard liner, the *Lusitania,* was torpedoed by a German U-boat U on 7 May 1915 and sank in eighteen minutes. It went down very quickly for such a large ship, just off the Old Head of Kinsale in County Cork. There were 761 survivors and 1198 people killed of the 1959 aboard. The sinking of the *Lusitania* turned public opinion in many countries against Germany and made America's entry into the war a stronger possibility. The doomed ship became a symbol in recruiting campaigns to illustrate why the war was being fought.

The *Lusitania* and her sister ship the *Mauretania* were two of the most luxurious ships built for the transatlantic passenger trade. Both ships held the Blue Riband speed record for a transatlantic crossing at different times in their careers.

The music industry reflected American society's gradual shift towards favouring war. The era was a golden age of popular music, a period when some of the greatest and most lasting musical ideas emerged and songs were produced at a rate that would make your head swim. The 'war to end all wars,' was a catalyst that produced even greater musical creativity and energy.

In 1914 the songs in vogue had titles such as 'Fido Is a Hot Dog Now', 'Rebecca of Sunny-Brook Farm', and 'Twelfth-Street Rag'. However, a few songs did relate to the war. 'Sister Susie's Sewing Shirts for Soldiers' and 'Goodbye, Little Girl, Goodbye' even dared to contemplate the possibility of a soldier going off to war.

When Charles Harris wrote 'When Angels Weep', the lyrics reminded those who listened to the song that they were all brothers and that they should pray for peace. Americans were divided into two groups: those backing Wilson's neutrality policy and those who believed America should help its friends in Europe. The position of songwriters on the question can clearly be seen through their music.

By 1915, the war was more to the fore in the consciousness of America and songs related to the war began to emerge. Most were anti-war, such as 'I Didn't Raise My Boy To Be a Soldier', or neutral, but a few patriotic songs began to emerge. Surprisingly, songs were still being published with German language titles: 'Wien, Du Stadt Meiner Traume' ('Vienna, City of My Dreams') in 1914 and 'Auf Wiedersehn' by Sigmund Romberg and Herbert Reynolds in 1915.

By 1916, more Americans were beginning to support the idea of going to war and by May of that year, hundreds of thousands of Americans were urging President Wilson and Congress to declare war. Although Wilson threatened Germany with war in April, he maintained neutrality for another full year. By 1917, it was becoming much more difficult to keep America out of the war. The unlimited submarine war was risking American lives and despite giving promises to act humanely, Germany escalated the war at sea and in April asked Japan and Mexico to join her as allies. With the war consuming the rest of the world and having the potential to reach the American border with Mexico, the United States finally declared war in April of 1917. Thus began a mobilisation and war effort that was unparalleled in history.

In a matter of just a few months America was training millions of soldiers and by June 1917, the first American troops arrived in France. American composers scrambled to write songs about the war and the music industry jumped into action claiming: 'Music will win the war'.

The Yanks brought their music to Europe with them, influencing a whole new audience and helping to make the appeal of music and song a more international affair.

Alfred Joyce Kilmer was one of the more famous Americans to join the war effort. He was born in New Brunswick, New Jersey, on 6 December 1886. As a young man he served as literary editor of the The Churchman, an Anglican newspaper, but converted to Catholicism towards the end of 1913.

When the US declared war on Germany in 1917, Kilmer was a family man with a wife and children and would not have been drafted. However he joined up as part of the New York National Guard and later transferred into the 165th Infantry, the old Fighting 69th. He assumed the position of senior regimental statistician.

Once in France, Kilmer quickly attained the rank of sergeant and was attached to the newly organised regimental intelligence staff as an observer. He spent many nights on patrol in no man's land gathering intelligence information but these excursions would not normally have occurred during combat operations. However he decided to put himself forward and was attached, during the battle of the Ourcq, to Major William Donovan as a replacement for his recently killed adjutant. Donovan seems to have had poor luck when it came to adjutants and a sniper's bullet ended the life of the very talented poet. He was only thirty-one.

The regiment's principal objective on that day had been the high ground of Muercy Farm. Major Donovan's two adjutants, Lieutenant Ames and Sergeant Kilmer, are buried side by side in a creek bed on that farm. Joyce Kilmer was awarded the French Croix de Guerre for bravery and Camp Kilmer in New Jersey is named for him.

Today Kilmer is best remembered for the poem 'Trees', published in 1914. The poem has a direct simplicity and wonderful charm as a song, for which Oscar Rasbach wrote the music:

Trees

Joyce Kilmer

I think that I shall never see,
A poem lovely as a tree.

A tree whose hungry mouth is pressed
Against the sweet earth's flowing breast;

A tree that looks at God all day,
And lifts her leafy arms to pray;

A tree that may in summer wear
A nest of robins in her hair;

Upon whose bosom snow has lain;
Who intimately lives with rain.

Poems are made by fools like me,
But only God can make a tree.

Prayer of a Soldier in France

Joyce Kilmer

An expression of Kilmer's s deep religious beliefs

My shoulders ache beneath my pack ,
(Lie easier, cross, upon His back).

I march with feet that burn and smart,
(Tread, holy feet, upon my heart).

Men shout at me who may not speak,
(They scourged Thy back and smote Thy cheek).

I may not lift a hand to clear,
My eyes of salty drops that sear.

(Then shall my fickle soul forget
Thy agony of bloody sweat?)

My rifle hand is stiff and numb,
(From Thy pierced palm red rivers come).

Lord, Thou didst suffer more for me,
Than all the hosts of land and sea.

So let me render back again,
This millionth of Thy gift. Amen.

When Angels Weep (Waltz of Peace)

Charles Harris

Glory to the Highest.
Peace on earth, goodwill to men.
Glory to the highest.
Hear our prayers ascending above.
Grant us sweet peace, oh, angel of love.
Bless all the nations on earth, we are brothers all.

Glory to the Highest.
Peace on earth, goodwill to men.
Glory to the highest.
Hear our prayers ascending above.
We are all pleading for this war to cease,
Let us dwell in love and peace.

Into the Night

Clara Edwards (1887-1974)

Silently into the night I go,
Into the fragrant night,
I know not where; the path is strange –
My weary steps are slow –
I do not find you there.

I turn my gaze toward the morning sun,
As from the east he comes thro' the dark and the dew;
The flowers lift their heads-the night is gone,
But where are you?

The countless weary steps I do not heed,
Tho' they be over land or boundless sea;
I care not where the road may lead,
If I but come again to thee.

Silently into the night I go,
Into the starry night of heavenly blue;
What matters where the road may lead,
If I but come again at last to you?

10

11/11/1918

Contrary to popular belief, the First World War didn't end on 11 November 1918 but on 28 June 1919, with the signing of the Treaty of Versailles. But all hostilities ceased at the eleventh hour on the eleventh day of the eleventh month of 1918. There were celebrations across Europe and the United States.

As we approach the centenary of the outbreak of the First World War the horrors of the trenches have gone from living memory into history. The last veterans have passed away but the battlegrounds of France and Belgium still slowly give up their secrets.

As recently as 2003, the remains of another British soldier was unearthed. Not much was left – a few bones, some buttons and a pair of boots – lying in the crater gouged by the shell that killed him. A team of British and Belgian archaeologists had been busy excavating a trench system near the village of St Jan. The site is on the route of a new motorway and the government in Brussels decreed that it should be thoroughly researched. In all, six British dead were recovered and, for once, a name was attached to one of them. William Storey was barely a man when he signed up for the Northumberland Fusiliers. From Blyth, Northumberland, he was part of a detachment from the regiment's 5th Battalion, that went into action on 26 October 1917. In all probability he was killed by a shell while waiting to go forward.

The battle in which Storey fought has become a byword for hellish and seemingly pointless sacrifice. Passchendaele was the third battle of Ypres, an attempt by Field Marshal Sir Douglas Haig to break the German line in the third year of the war. It was in the same campaign that Dubliner Lawrence Kelly was killed on 31 July 1917

Pillars honour the dead of various divisions in the Irish commemorative park in Messines, Belgium

A pillar marking the dead of thirty-two counties in the Irish commemorative park in Messines, Belgium

The campaign that began in July 1917 ended in November when the British advance ground to a halt in a sea of mud. The thousands of names on the memorials and headstones that dot the flat, often waterlogged landscape stand as testament to its failure.

Before the excavation, William Storey had no grave. He is listed as missing and his name is among to the 34,888 names engraved on the enormous memorial at Tyne Cot, near Ypres.

The remains of a Canadian soldier that were discovered during construction work in France eight years ago have also been identified. The identity of Private Thomas Lawless was established after extensive work by forensic specialists and researchers using isotope signatures from his teeth. Genetic testing using a DNA sample from a relative in Canada confirmed that the remains were those of Thomas Lawless, who was born on 11 April 1889 and emigrated from Dublin to Calgary, Alberta, with members of his family. He enlisted in the 49th Battalion of the Canadian Expeditionary Forces in 1915.

Because the fighting was so intense here over such a long period, the whole of this area is one huge cemetery. The remains of hundreds of thousands of men are still out there waiting to be found.

Likewise in Gallipoli there are human remains still partially covered in the rough terrain. Many of the marked graves simply have the inscription 'believed to be buried in the cemetery' or 'known unto God'

There are German graves in Flanders and Gallipoli, along with those of their Turkish allies and graves of the soldiers of other nations who participated. After the war only a small amount of land was allowed for German cemeteries in Flanders, so most of the unknown soldiers are buried in what is known as a *Kameraden Grab* ('comrades grave'), normally with eight soldiers per plot. The largest and most significant cemetery is at Langemark, where more than three thousand of the student soldiers who took part in the battle of Langemark during October and November 1914 are interred in *Der*

Studentenfriedhof. Since the 1930s many of those buried in smaller graveyards dotted around the region were moved to Langemark, where the bodies of more than 10,000 soldiers have their final resting place.

When the war finally came to a close, the war to end all wars, it had still not resolved the issues to any great degree. The German troops marched home with their arms intact and the whole bloody mess started again just over twenty years later.

The last combat veteran died very recently. Claude Choules, who had served in the British Royal Navy, died in his sleep in Sydney in May 2011. I'm sure he found it extremely difficult to sleep for the noise of the guns during the war, while after the war the silence probably kept him awake on many a long night as he remembered the horrors that he had shared with his comrades in arms many decades before.

The German cemetery in Langemark, Belgium

Statues bear silent witness in the German cemetery of Langemark

O Del Mio Amato Ben

Stefano Danoudy (1879-1925)

Oh, lost enchantment of my dearly beloved!
Far from my eyes is he,
Who was, to me, glory and pride!
Now through the empty rooms,
I always seek him and call him,
With a heart full of hopes.
But I seek in vain, I call in vain!
And the weeping is so dear to me,
That with weeping alone I nourish my heart.

It seems to me, without him, sad everywhere.
The day seems like night to me;
The fire seems cold to me.
If, however, I sometimes hope,
To give myself to another cure,
One thought alone torments me:
But without him, what shall I do?
To me, life seems a vain thing
Without my beloved.

Free Download on www.londubh.ie

Some of the songs featured in *March Away My Brothers*, performed by the author, are available as a free download. Please go to www.londubh.ie and follow the link to download the songs.